IMPORTING
for the
SMALL
BUSINESS

IMPORTING for the SMALL BUSINESS

SECOND EDITION

Mag Morris

**KOGAN
PAGE**

Acknowledgements
The author thanks the following organisations for kind permission to reproduce copyright material: Behring International; British-Portuguese Chamber of Commerce; Formecon Services Ltd; German Chamber of Commerce; Hong Kong Chamber of Commerce; London Chamber of Commerce and Industry; Spanish Chamber of Commerce. Figures 6.7, 6.8 and 8.1 are Crown copyright and reproduced with the permission of the Controller of Her Majesty's Stationery Office.

First published in Great Britain in 1985 by
Kogan Page Ltd, 120 Pentonville Road, London N1 9JN
Second edition 1988

British Library Cataloguing in Publication Data

Morris, Mag
   Importing for the small business — 2nd ed.
   1. Great Britain — Importing by small firms
   I. Title
   658.8'48

   ISBN 1-85091-648-9

Printed and bound in Great Britain by
Biddles Ltd, Guildford and King's Lynn

Contents

List of Illustrations

Chapter 1

The Import Decision

Importing, or buying goods or services from other countries, is often held not to be in the best interests of Britain. Importers are, therefore, frequently accused of spending precious foreign currency, failing to support British industry and encouraging people to prefer goods and services produced in other countries, thereby helping to increase unemployment, and so on.

Exporters, by contrast, are constantly exhorted to sell more overseas, and are held up as the saviours of their country. Moreover, they are actively encouraged by free government help at all levels, even to being promised awards and honours if they are successful. Without our exporters' efforts, we are told, Britain would not survive.

Yet if Britain did not import she would hardly be able to export, since any country which buys from Britain must also sell to us, in order to earn the sterling with which to pay our exporters.

The importance of import in international trade

An increase in international trade is essential if there is to be any real prosperity anywhere in the world, and if the gap between rich and poor nations is ever to be narrowed, it follows that both exports from and imports into Britain and other countries have to be increased. Assuming that you have decided to begin importing, or to expand your import business because you cannot get the sort of goods you want in the UK; or you have found that the price is too high locally for what you need; or you have located a market for a particular product, such as exotic foods from the Far East, knitted goods from South America, tableware from Yugoslavia, lighting fixtures from Italy, jeans and sweatshirts from the USA, you must from the outset get rid of any feeling of guilt that you are not acting in the best interests of your country. Remember that it does not make economic sense to encourage inefficient local production by limiting imports. Nor does it do any good to restrict the choice of the consumer, as this only results in less demand for such goods, and as demand decreases so will supply. Besides, Britain has too many treaties with other countries, such as those in the European Community (EC) and through the General Agreement on Tariffs and Trade (GATT), to make import controls feasible. It is not unpatriotic to import, merely sound economic sense.

You should approach importing on the basis that almost everyone in the world is both a seller and a buyer, and that by buying you are enabling others to sell. Importing is the corollary of exporting and a knowledge of one greatly increases a knowledge of the other. To export successfully you should know how to import, so to be a good importer you should be familiar with how exporters operate.

In addition, note that exporters are taught that if they want to obtain business they should consider buying in return. Many successful companies offer, for example, to buy raw materials when their customers place orders for manufactured goods with them. This is known as countertrade.

Another similarity between importers and exporters is that both need to know something of the idiosyncrasies of their customers or suppliers, who will be of different nationalities, speaking a variety of languages, and operating in ways often quite different from those in Britain. With over 200 currencies in the world the means of exchanging goods or services by the use of money will be different from those at home. A successful exporter studies his buyers, and as an importer you should also study your suppliers, and the way they do business.

This book is based on successful experience of importing both in Britain and overseas. Examples of successes and failures will be quoted. But it cannot cover the whole of such a huge subject and practical experience will be needed before any business, large or small, can hope to know it all. It should, however, give you the essentials for a successful importing business.

On being a customer

An importer is a customer who buys and pays for goods or services supplied from other countries.

When you buy you can, to a major degree, dictate the terms, refusing to buy if these terms are not to your liking. A long-standing weakness of British industry has been its unwillingness to consider the customer, many companies making goods and then expecting people overseas to buy them. The Americans, the Japanese, the Europeans and others have now exposed the folly of such an approach, and shown that the way to successful international trade is to find out what people want, and then supply it on reasonable but profitable terms. As an importer, therefore, you will have to deal with professional suppliers, so you will only obtain the goods or services you require on your terms if you are equally professional in your dealings with those who export to you. The more professional you are as a customer, the better will be the terms on which you import.

This may not, however, always be the case. For example, you may find there is only one supplier of the goods you require. In Mombasa an importer had a demand for a certain drug, made by only one US manufacturer. The Kenyan importer had to agree to his terms or go without. Oil has been the classic example of supply and price problems for buyers for several years, because the OPEC countries have dictated the price and terms on which oil may be bought, even to insisting on payment in American dollars, thereby nearly bankrupting small countries who had to have oil, but lacked foreign currency.

Another problem which may arise is shortage of stock. A certain type of black coffee was in great demand in West Germany, but the People's Republic of the Congo was able to supply only half the quantities required. The West Germans had to wait for their supplies, which did not endear them to their customers. So you must learn to be a good customer, and one who will be supplied in preference to others. Part of the aim of this book is to show you how to become a better customer.

One of the pleasures of being an importer is that you will be welcomed in other countries when you go there to buy. We have found visiting Japan as a buyer much more pleasurable than going there to sell, although dealing with the Japanese is, as some of you may know, an art which takes years to acquire.

We mentioned countertrade earlier. As a buyer you will often be in quite a strong position to sell, because you can say, in effect, 'I will buy from you if I can also sell to you.' We do not suggest that all importers should automatically become exporters, but if a suitable opportunity arises there would be no reason to refuse to sell at the same time as you agree to buy.

The use of certain terms

At this point it may be helpful if we define certain terms used in this book. Moreover, it is useful to know who is speaking to whom, so that in the first place, when we use the word 'we' this indicates the author of this book and her associates, all of whom are experienced importers and speak from practical experience.

Second, the word 'you' will be used to denote the reader, that is, the small businessman or woman who is anxious to start importing, or expand existing importing activities.

Third, as regards people in this country and overseas there are several words in common use, such as importers and exporters, buyers and sellers, customers and suppliers, and consignees and consignors. They all have the same general meaning, but there are differences between them, so for the sake of clarity we will use them as follows:

Importers we will take to mean those who do some form of importing, that is, buying goods or services which are not of British origin, irrespective of their source of supply. An *exporter* will denote someone selling goods or services outside his country, however or wherever he may supply these goods.

A *buyer* will be one who buys, pays for and uses the goods, while the *seller* is one who supplies and receives payment for the goods.

On the other hand, a *customer* will be used to denote one who buys the goods but who may then resell them to someone else, and is not necessarily the final or end user. A *supplier* is the person who sells to the customer, whether or not he produces the goods, because in many cases, as you will see, suppliers are not manufacturers.

A *consignee* is the person to whom the imported goods are sent, not necessarily the same as the buyer, while the *consignor* is the person sending the goods, not always the same person as the seller. The reason for using these two words in these contexts is that they appear on most transport documents, and the use of other people to despatch and receive goods in the import trade is, in the case of small businesses, likely to be widespread.

To talk about an importer as such can, therefore, be misleading, because a great deal will depend on what kind of an importer you propose to be, a point to be considered later in this chapter.

What to import

It is assumed that you will already have decided what goods or services you wish to import, because you are already established in a certain line of business. However, you may wish to learn what goods are likely to be worth importing, and from which countries these are most likely to come.

As a start, study the UK *Trade and Navigation Accounts*, published monthly and yearly in summary form by HM Stationery Office which show all the goods imported into the UK, from which country they have come, and the value of each. As you may know, manufactured goods make up some 50 per cent of all British imports, with an additional 15 per cent of food, drink and tobacco, and 15 per cent of raw materials. The remainder is made up of oil and miscellaneous items.

The goods which seem to show most promise for the future are convenience foods, drinks, fashion goods, toys, textiles, vehicles, electronic goods of all kinds, and anything connected with the do-it-yourself market. New forms of finished materials will be sought, especially those available in a semi-finished state. Britain has now to import many of her traditional exports, as developing nations start to produce their own goods and sell them back to us, while we concentrate on selling overseas the more sophisticated manufactured goods the developing nations cannot yet produce. This is a continuous process of change in the patterns of UK exports and imports.

The countries which are most likely to supply these goods are, first, North America, Japan and Western Europe of the developed nations, and then the more developing nations of Hong Kong, Malaysia, Taiwan and South Korea, and some South American nations. Clothing and fashion goods are their likely exports to us, with the developed nations also supplying manufactures. Raw materials will come from African and Central and South American countries. We suggest you study the pattern of British imports in relation to the business you are in, in order to obtain some idea of the best sources of supply for yourselves.

Legally you are not allowed to import anything into Britain without an import licence issued by the Department of Trade and Industry — by reason of the Import of Goods (Control) Order of 1954 — apart from samples and goods to be repaired, along with household goods if you are coming here to live. In practice most goods are imported under Open General Licence, although an entry permit is required before HM Customs, who are responsible for all imports, will clear the goods. There are, of course, certain goods which do require an import licence such as drugs, arms etc, but you are unlikely to be concerned with these.

The procedures to be followed, and the documents needed, are explained later in this book, but at this stage you should obtain a copy of *Croner's Reference Book for Importers*. It is updated monthly so that you may keep up to date with all changes in the import regulations as they occur. Import controls for goods coming into Britain are not at present severe because free trade is allowed with other members of the EC and countries associated with the Community, as well as with many other nations under the General Agreement on Tariffs and Trade. There are, however, some restrictions imposed by customs, such as those on plants and animals, but these are all set out in *Croner's*. There will, of course, be many regulations imposed in your own trade area, such as labelling, marking, the use of certain raw materials etc, which you should already know, and with which your suppliers overseas will need to conform, many of these regulations being imposed under EC directives.

Customs and/or excise duties may have to be paid on goods entering the country, while value added tax (VAT) will be charged where applicable at the same rate as for home-produced goods.

If this begins to sound formidable, do not despair because any good clearing agent will attend to the details for you. Your task at this stage is to spot the opportunities in your own or a related line of business, and thus give a sense of direction to your importing activities.

Your next task is to decide what kind of an importer you wish to be: one who imports indirectly from suppliers in the UK, or one who imports directly from suppliers overseas.

Indirect importing

Let's start by looking at the easier way — that is by using the services of someone in this country who does the actual importing, so you are in fact importing indirectly. There are three main ways to do this:

First, you can import through a wholesaler or import merchant, who will bring the goods into the country, then sell them to you. Wholesalers or merchants take all the risks of importing the goods; they arrange the transport and insurance, and handle the documents involved, so as far as you are concerned the transaction is basically like buying on the home market. Wholesalers may hold stock, in which case the goods should be readily available. They often specialise in particular trading areas and sometimes in particular products. They are not tied to any special supplier overseas, so are free to get the best deal they can, and you gain the benefit of their experience.

Second, you can import through the import agent of the overseas supplier, assuming he has one. There are two kinds of agent. One is the commission agent, who takes orders from you; he then sends them to his overseas principal, who supplies the goods direct to you. His profit will come from the commission paid to him by his principal. The other kind of agent is the distributor, who holds stocks and sells direct to you for his own account. He will have paid for the goods he has imported, and will make his profit by adding it to the price which he has paid for the goods, including all charges involved in bringing them to the UK.

For example, if you buy a foreign car, say a Datsun or a Fiat, from a distributor, he will have bought the car, hold stocks of spare parts, and probably service and repair the car. But if you bought a foreign car (eg a Lamborghini or Ferrari) from an agent, he will order the car for you from the manufacturer, and import it, but will not hold stocks. You pay the manufacturer, and he pays a commission to the agent.

Third, you can import through the UK subsidiary of the overseas supplier, if he has one, in which case the UK subsidiary company will deal with your order, arrange the price and see you are a satisfied customer. So when you buy in this way there is no more commercial risk than in purchasing on the domestic market, with no problems of language, currency, import duties, customs clearance, quotas, restrictions or foreign exchange fluctuations. It is exactly like buying locally, except that you are buying foreign goods, and, to that extent, are importing.

However, there are some disadvantages when you import in this way, and buy from any of these people. Extra costs are involved, because the man in the middle who is taking all the risks will charge for this. Therefore, the final cost to you as the customer will be increased by the amount of the agent's commission or the distributor's mark-up. You have no direct contact with your suppliers, so it may be difficult to build up any long-term trading relationship, which would make you into a valued customer. In addition, as an importer you may have some difficulties in negotiating particular requirements or improving on the price quoted, or obtaining better payment terms than those offered. To achieve this you need, as a customer, to be in close direct touch with your suppliers.

Further information about wholesalers, import merchants, commission agents, distributors etc can be obtained from the British Importers Confederation, 69 Cannon Street, London EC4N 5AB (01-248 4444), and various directories such as the *Directory of British Importers* or the *Directory of British Clothing and Textile Importers*, which contain the following kind of entry:

> HART LTD. 561 East Road, Walthamstow, London E3. Tel 659 9203. Importer/Wholesaler. Import: Household giftware, artistic frames and table lamps; embroidered household linen; furnishing fabrics. Buy from any suitable supplier. Import from India, Pakistan, Taiwan.

> HEAVEN-SENT LTD. 35 Station Road, Bridgend. Tel 424 55432. Manufacturer/Wholesaler/Importer. Import: Leather finishing products for the tanning industry. High quality small leather goods, soft luggage and travel goods. Buy from any suitable supplier. Import from France, Italy, Spain.

So that is one way of being an importer. You will not have the hassle of dealing direct with foreign suppliers, or chasing all over the world looking for goods to import. It is a good way to start.

Direct importing

However, you may prefer to buy directly from exporters overseas, so why not do it yourself and import from suppliers as a direct customer? This means you will have to find suppliers overseas and deal directly with them. The main advantage of doing it yourself is that the final cost of the goods may be lower because no middleman will be involved, which could lead to a greater turnover for you and also greater profit (a word more about which will be said in Chapter 2). You may also get better terms and better treatment from your suppliers overseas because you can demonstrate to them that you are a highly professional buyer.

Having identified what sort of goods or services you wish to buy directly, your next step is to find the best suppliers. The sources available to you of this kind of information are numerous, some of which have already been mentioned, but here is a list you may find useful:

1. The Department of Trade and Industry have not only official figures of what is imported into Britain but also information on what is most suitable, where the sources of supply can be found etc.
2. All the embassies and high commissions of other countries have special commercial sections to promote their country's exports, and will be glad to suggest to you goods and services which can be supplied, also the names of possible suppliers.
3 Some countries even have trade councils which deal directly with British importers (the Hong Kong Trade Development Council, the Irish Export Board etc).
4. There are specialist organisations in some countries, eg the British Overseas Trade Group for Israel and the Netherlands-British Chamber of Commerce.
5. The Developing Countries Trade Agency is a government-assisted organisation which can answer trade enquiries.
6. Your local Chamber of Commerce can provide information about overseas suppliers, and they are often contacted by foreign exporters looking for market opportunities.
7. The major clearing banks, through their trade development sections, receive many enquiries from overseas firms and can often provide possible sources of supply.
8. Trade journals and directories are available in many public libraries or in the library section of the Chamber of Commerce.
9. Many foreign exporters attend trade fairs and exhibitions in Britain, and seeing them there gives you the chance to examine what they have to offer on the spot.
10. Members of trade missions will often be entertained in the Chamber of Commerce, which is an excellent opportunity to meet the suppliers personally.

Much of this information is free (notably from the Chamber of Commerce if you are a member), and you may be able to find out as much as you need to know this way.

Depending on what your budget will stand, and where your possible suppliers are, you might also consider visiting the markets. But be sure to do your homework thoroughly before you go, and then you may well obtain a great deal of valuable information that you might not get from other sources. If you want to learn the essentials about a country before going there, get hold of a copy of the relevant 'Hints to Exporters', issued by the British Overseas Trade Board.

But whatever the type of goods you want to import, or wherever you need to buy them, there will be problems to be faced, which you would probably not have to cope with if you bought them on the home market. These problems will be:

Sources of supply

Which parts of the world are the most promising as sources of supply for the goods you want? Do we have any special arrangements in Britain for importing free of duty from the EC? Are there places where rates of import duty are lower than others? Where do you start looking, and how do you evaluate suppliers?

What guarantee will you have that the goods will be of the right quality and exactly as you ordered? Will they be delivered on time, or at all? Will samples be sent? What languages do you use in correspondence? And if there is a conflict over the contract, under which law would it be judged? In Chapter 2 we will attempt to answer these questions.

Delivery

What options do you have on transport? Should the goods be sent to you by sea, air, road, rail or parcel post? Do you want the goods delivered to your warehouse, with your supplier taking full responsibility from his door to your door, or should you organise at least some of the transport yourself, and handle some of the documentation? And if you do decide to take some of this responsibility, how are you going to set about arranging the transport and preparing the documents? Chapter 2 deals with terms of delivery, and Chapter 3 with transportation and documentation.

Official requirements

Will your supplier need an export licence and will your goods need an import licence? What about quotas, if they apply to your types of goods (a point especially relevant to products such as textiles)? Will the goods conform to British standards, and how will they have to be marked or labelled, especially if they have to conform to safety standards? Chapter 5 deals with customs and excise and Chapter 7 with quotas.

Price

This is a crucial point, because you wish to buy at the lowest price consistent with the quality etc of the goods, but how do you know what that lowest price will be, since your supplier will clearly want the highest price he can get from you?

Then what about additional costs such as transport, insurance, inland delivery, agents' fees, customs duties, VAT and bank charges, because all these will have to be paid by you in the end? And do you know if any of them will be included in the price you are quoted?

Do you pay in your supplier's currency or sterling, and how do you actually pay? Even more important, *when* do you have to pay and what guarantees, if any, will your supplier require before he sends you the goods? After all, he may not trust you very far so what happens then?

Finally, you have to arrive at a total cost of the goods to you in this country (this is often called the landed cost) which will either be satisfactory, if you plan to use the goods yourself, or allow you a reasonable profit if you resell them. It sounds all right, but can you be sure it will work out that way? Chapter 2 discusses prices, while terms of payment are dealt with in Chapter 4, with Chapter 7 detailing customs duties.

Perhaps this seems a formidable list of problems, but answers will be forthcoming all the way through this book. So now make up your mind whether you wish to start by importing indirectly or whether you will also buy directly from overseas, and make sure you know exactly what you will do with the goods when you get them. Also decide a maximum cost to you for the goods, beyond which it will not be worth your while buying.

Your next step is to consider how to place your orders, and in particular the criteria you will use to determine the prices and terms under which you will buy, which we will deal with in the next chapter.

Chapter 2

Quotations, Orders, Contracts and Insurance

The two most important decisions which you, as an importer, will have to take concern, first, the value and quality of the goods you decide to buy; and second, the price you are prepared to pay for them. We shall not in this book try to help you with your choice of goods, assuming you are already sufficiently knowledgeable about what you wish to import either to use yourself, or to resell to others. We shall, however, concentrate on helping you to learn how to decide the price and terms of payment or, to put it another way, the cost to you of those goods. Price and cost are not entirely synonymous, since cost can be greater than price. For example, the price you pay for some wool in Australia may well include only the actual wool, whereas to that price you would have to add the cost of transport, packing, insurance, customs duty etc, before you could say what the final cost of the wool in a usable or resaleable condition was to you. And even then, as you probably know, if the wool were to remain unsold in stock, its cost to you would be even greater.

Initial prices or costs

While your supplier will quote you a price, it is better if you consider this as a cost to yourself. Moreover, there are several factors which will affect the price your supplier will quote, and these are:

First, *when you will place the order* — because no supplier likes to guarantee his prices for delivery overseas for more than about six months ahead. So when you are considering placing an order or asking for a quotation, state clearly when you intend to buy, other things being equal. You are likely to obtain a better price if you clearly intend to buy immediately, because a seller is always anxious, unless he is over-committed, to have a firm order in his hand.

Second, the price to you, which is the basis of your costs,

will depend in most cases on *the quantity you are going to buy.*
This is because the cost to the supplier tends to decrease as the
quantity rises. Of course, this is true only to a limited extent,
but if you were going to buy, say, a transformer from Italy,
and you decide you can do with three transformers, if you
place an order for three at the same time the Italian supplier
will probably quote you a lower price for each than if you
ordered one at a time. In most trades there are some forms of
quantity discount.

Third, a great deal will depend on *when you are going to pay,*
and in what way. This point will be considered again in Chapter 4
but, as you know, when anyone pays cash there is usually a
discount. If you are buying wine in France, and you pay in
French francs now, you will pay less than if you offer some
other currency to be paid at some time in the future.

So before you decide to ask for a quotation, be prepared
to state clearly when you propose to place an order if the
terms are satisfactory; how much you intend buying; and when
and how you propose to pay. This should enable the supplier
to quote you his lowest price, unless he is short of stock and
does not really want the business. In this case you have to
accept his terms, but one hopes this is not a frequent occur-
rence. At this stage you can ask a supplier for a quotation.

Quotations

As a prospective customer it is best if you are quite decisive
about the form you want the quotation to take, especially as
an exporter is always taught that a quotation should be in the
form requested by the importer. The points you should include
when requesting a quotation are as follows:

1. Identify yourself clearly, with all relevant details as to
   how you can be contacted.
2. Explain who you are, what business you are in, whether
   you plan to buy to use or resell, whether you cover the
   whole of the UK, who your bankers are and any other information which will convince your overseas supplier that
   you are a serious enquirer and worth taking his time over.
3. Define the goods or services you propose to buy and
   explain where you heard of or saw them.
4. State how you would wish the goods to be packed and
   marked.
5. State the quantities you have in mind, possibly hinting at

    larger quantities if the price and terms are to your satis-
faction.

6. State when you propose to buy and when you require delivery.
7. Define the terms of delivery you wish used (see below).
8. State whether you wish to handle all or part of the transport, insurance etc (see Chapter 3 for transport, and later in this chapter for insurance).
9. State any conditions of purchase you may have, especially if the goods will require any special labelling or packaging, in order to conform with any particular regulations in this country.

So far as possible you should have a fairly standardised form of request for a quotation, because this will help you, when you receive several quotations from different suppliers, to compare them and decide on the most suitable. Besides, a clear workman-like request for a quotation is more likely to receive instant attention than one which looks as though you are not serious. Quotations are not always dealt with in rotation, but in what suppliers feel is their order of importance, as many of you probably do with your customers in this country. It is the difficult or incomprehensible letters that end up in the pending tray.

You must also establish in which language you wish to receive a quotation, and to conduct correspondence with your prospective suppliers. Although English is the most widely used language in the world for commerce, by no means every-one is able to write or speak it, so if you wish to obtain the best terms from your suppliers maybe it would help if you were prepared to use their language. In these days of multi-racial offices, language is often not as much of a problem as it used to be, and many companies, even the smaller ones, find that they have people who can at least translate from some other languages. Yet even if you cannot cope with Farsi from Iran, Amharic from Ethiopia or Mandarin from China, and you are asking for quotations from these countries, make it clear when a local language quotation will be acceptable, on the basis that you can have it translated in the UK without great expense.

The best way for a quotation to be made is in the form of a pro-forma invoice, since this shows clearly what you would expect to see in the way of an invoice if you were to place the order. It should include all the additional costs likely to be incurred, with the exception of your local unloading charges, customs duties and local transport charges which you can easily estimate yourself.

Make sure that each request for a quotation is individually signed, and that the signature is legible or the name clearly shown, because people overseas like dealing with a named person in a company. Moreover, make sure the title of the person concerned is stated, again because many people use titles and are impressed by them. In Britain we are not as conscious of titles as people are in Germany, Switzerland or Sweden, while in parts of South America the grander the title you have the more people wish to deal with you. One interesting gimmick used by a British importer is putting in capital letters, at the foot of a request for a quotation, the words 'PLEASE MARK YOUR QUOTATION FOR THE PERSONAL ATTENTION OF H MAYHEW, MANAGING DIRECTOR', because he has found that his requests are never ignored and are usually answered by return. There is, as we are sure you appreciate, a great art in flattering people in commerce, so if you can personalise your buying, then you are more likely to be treated as a favoured customer and may be given preferential attention and service.

Terms of delivery

In order that quotations can be in a clearly understandable form the price quoted by the exporter, or the cost to the importer, should state three things:

1. What is included in the price quoted.
2. Where delivery of the goods takes place.
3. Where possession of the goods passes from the exporter into the hands of the importer. (*Note.* This question of possession is not to be confused with ownership which depends ultimately on payment.)

If you buy a packet of cigarettes in a tobacconist's, all you get for your money is one packet of cigarettes. You take the packet away with you, so delivery takes place at the shop, at which point the cigarettes are in your possession. If you dropped them in the street *you* would lose, not the shopkeeper who sold them to you. But if you bought a suite of furniture the shop would probably deliver it to your home, depending on how far that was, and the terms under which you bought. And if the suite was damaged in transit, the store would be liable.

23

Clearly, when you are selling to customers overseas, and buying from suppliers in other countries, it would be tedious to spell out all these conditions every time you made or received a quotation. For this reason, for many years there have been in existence what are called Terms of Delivery, which have now become widely accepted, and codified by a set of rules which have the force of law in most countries. More of that later, but while there are about 15 of these terms, there are seven which are mostly used in international trade today:

Ex Works. Delivery takes place at the factory of the seller, where possession changes hands, and included in the price is merely the cost of the goods. The only obligation of the seller is to provide an invoice, along with the goods, although it is generally assumed the goods should be adequately packed.

FOR, FOT. These both refer to rail and mean Free on Rail and Free on Truck, delivery taking place at the nearest railway station, where the buyer takes possession of the goods. Transport to the station is included in the price, along with an invoice and a railway document, but no freight etc.

FOB. This means Free on Board, and is the most commonly used term in the import/export business. Delivery takes place as the goods pass over the side of the ship's rail, though title to them may not pass until payment has been made. The exporter pays all loading charges as well as transport to the docks, and also provides all the necessary shipping documents including the bill of lading. He does not pay the sea freight, nor does he insure the goods. The buyer pays the freight and is responsible for insurance, and must advise the seller of the name of the ship on which the goods are to travel, giving sufficient time for this to be done.

FOB is the most common of all terms because it enables the buyer to nominate the carrier, and by using ships of his own country he can save foreign exchange, as well as pay for insurance locally.

If goods are shipped by air (FOA = FOB Airport) the exchange of the goods takes place when they are handed over to the air carrier or his agents, which will normally be at the airport. But the exporter will probably nominate that airport, as he will probably also nominate the sea port to which he will deliver.

C&F, CIF. These mean Cost and Freight/Cost, Insurance and Freight, and the exchange takes place at the sea port or airport of destination, so to these quotations the exporter will usually add 'CIF London'. When the ship arrives at London docks the importer takes over, paying the unloading charges, customs duty if any, and inland transport charges. The exporter will have paid the sea freight and insurance under CIF, but with C&F the buyer pays the insurance.

Franco Domicile. This term means that the seller pays all charges right up to the buyer's warehouse, and it is therefore a delivered price. It does not include customs duty, unless this is specifically stated. It will normally be shown as Franco Domicile London, or wherever the importer requests. As with FOB and upwards, all the documents will be provided free by the seller. However, *Incoterms* (see below) define it as DDP.

It is assumed that adequate packing is provided at all times by the seller, but where special packing is required the seller should state something like 'Packing extra at cost' if he proposes to charge for it. As an importer, always query packing costs before placing the order.

As a customer it is up to you to decide under which term of delivery you propose to buy, and to ask for a quotation accordingly. Obviously the price or cost to you will vary with the quotation, ex works being the cheapest, and franco domicile duty paid the most expensive. Your choice must depend on how far you wish to be involved with the transport, insurance etc, or whether you wish your seller to do it for you. We examine transport problems in the next chapter, which may help you to decide for which term of delivery you require a quotation. But be sure to specify one on your request for a quotation.

We said earlier that these terms of delivery have been codified; this has been done by the International Chamber of Commerce under the title of *Incoterms*. These define each term legally, and if you add 'Incoterms 1980' to the term for which you require a quotation, you are saying that you will interpret that term according to the ICC rules, the latest revision being in 1980. This makes it easier should any dispute arise with your supplier, which can always happen. Notice that almost all countries accept Incoterms, but in the USA there are different interpretations of them, so be careful when buying from the Americans to get a definition from them of, say, FOB, which is rather different from FOB elsewhere.

You will now appreciate that according to which term of

delivery is used the price will vary, although the actual final cost to you will be much the same, since as the buyer you pay for all the charges such as transport, insurance, documentation etc. But then, the customer always pays for everything in the end.

Finally, there is the question of whether you ask for a quotation in your own currency, say sterling, or leave it to your supplier to quote in his own currency, say US dollars. This can be a complicated problem, but to put it simply, if you have a quotation in sterling, then your US supplier takes the risk that when you pay him he may not get as much for the sterling, when he sells it for dollars, as when the quotation was made. On the other hand, if the rate of exchange went in favour of the dollar he might get more. If, however, you have a quotation in your supplier's currency, say US dollars, then you will take the risk that when you come to pay for the goods the rate of exchange may have altered, so that you have to pay more when you sell the sterling for dollars to pay the supplier. Alternatively, you might gain should the rate of exchange go the other way.

From your point of view it is better to pay in your own currency, ie sterling, as then you always know exactly what you have to pay, and you should ask for your quotations to be made in sterling. Your supplier may well prefer to quote in his own currency, and if he does then you must be careful to guard against loss when you come to pay. We do not recommend that you gamble on the exchange in the hopes of gaining, but you should insure yourself against loss by an arrangement with the banks, which is explained in Chapter 4.

Orders/Contracts

On receipt of the quotations you will have to decide whether to buy, and if so from which supplier, at which stage you will send out the order. This will be an invitation to the supplier to make a contract with you. On the order you should state clearly the details of the goods you are ordering, including quantities, prices, terms of delivery, and all the other details you mentioned on the request for a quotation. You must also include your own conditions of purchase which will take precedence over your supplier's conditions of sale.

In English law you will have the first part of a contract as soon as your supplier accepts your order, but his acceptance should agree with your order in every detail to make it a valid contract. Do not make any assumptions and make sure every detail is agreed between you and your supplier, because disputed contracts from overseas suppliers are nearly always caused by one or other of the two parties assuming one thing, with the other side claiming they never agreed to it.

It is best if you can agree with your supplier that the contract is subject to English (or Scottish) law. If not, he might agree to the adoption of the Uniform Laws of the International Sale of Goods (Cmnd 5029), either in whole or part. There is no worldwide law of contract, but these Uniform Laws are the nearest to it.

In your contract it will be implied that both sides must cooperate to arrive at a satisfactory completion of the deal, ie that the supplier will supply the goods as specified, and that the buyer will accept and pay for them. The supplier must deliver to the place specified in the contract and he must also provide any necessary documents relating to the contract, although this will be subject to any special arrangements made for payment, and the delivery of the documents to the buyer will be made in various ways according to how payment is to be made, as shown in Chapter 4. The supplier must also hand over title and ownership to the goods as required.

As a buyer you must take delivery of the goods as and when notified by the seller that they are ready. You must pay the agreed price on the due date using the method of payment specified in the contract. You can, however, reject the goods if they are not in accordance with the contract, and you must examine them promptly, notifying your supplier of their rejection as soon as possible. As you will see below, you must also examine them promptly if you need to make an insurance claim.

The supplier can ask for the contract to be amended, for instance if he wants you to accept a later delivery date, and you can either accept or refuse. In the same way you can ask for the place of delivery to be altered which your supplier can accept or refuse.

The overriding consideration, and this is what any dispute over a contract will be judged on, is the intention of you and your supplier. So make it clear in the contract exactly what your intention is, and check that you see clearly the intention of your supplier. If both are similar, then you will have a good contract, on which it is unlikely any disputes will arise.

Insurance

Having considered safeguarding yourself against any loss on the

IMPORT DATA FOLDER	PURCHASE ORDER No. or CONTRACT No.	1730/99

OVERSEAS SUPPLIER (Consignor)	SUPPLIER'S REP./AGENT (or Confirming House)	Date Order Placed
Taiwan Industries Incorporated P.O. Box 350 Taipei Taiwan		1 February 198..
		Our Internal Ref.
		ALB/632/1A
		Time Difference
Contact Name: Lee Chang Chinn	Contact Name	+ 8 (GMT)
Tel. No. 68932 - 5078 Telex Leechi 6739	Tel. No. Telex	− Hrs.

BUYER	CONSIGNEE (and Delivery Address if different to Buyer)	Import Licence No.
Gibb Sunn and Mayhew plc Model Importers Smith Way London 1AA 2BC Tel 01 778 605		
		Payment Terms
		Irrevocable L/C
		L/C Number & Dates
Contact Name M. Sheen	Contact Name	22980/GBA
Tel. No. 01 778 605 Telex 56789 Gib	Tel. No. Telex	1/8/19../1/11/19.

ARRIVAL PORT CLEARING AGENT	TERMS OF DELIVERY (Incoterms)		INSURANCE		
Acme Forwarders 112 Highover Street London EC2A AB4	CIF		Seller	Tick relevant box	✓
	Loading Point	Keelong Taiwan	Buyer		
	Discharge Point	London	Insured Value		
	Vessel/Flight No.	Chamcom 7	FREIGHT		
	Container No.		Prepaid	Tick relevant box	✓
	B/L - AWB No.	198			
Contact Name K. Smith	Est. Arrival Date	23.10.198..@	Collect		
Tel. No. 01 6264 89 Telex 32311 Acme	Act. Arrival Date	@			

(see back page)

DETAILS OF GOODS PURCHASED

500 "Morgan" Series 12B/TCA	£1200.00
500 "Morris" Series 1WD/BTN	£1500.00
250 "Davidsons" Series 561, cat. no. 3252/76/MT	£875.00

Freight and insurance at cost

Figure 2.1 *Import data folder*

foreign exchange, you should next insure yourself against the consequences of the goods you have bought from overseas being lost or damaged in transit. You may or may not handle any or all of the transport of these goods, as will be discussed in the next chapter, but whether you or your supplier arranges the transport, you should make sure they are insured.

Although there is no law which says goods must be insured you, as a buyer, would be unwise to take the risk that goods you have ordered, and possibly paid for, might be damaged or lost on the way. Equally, however, your supplier would be unwilling to take those risks since he might also lose financially. So it is customary in international trade for goods sent from one country to another to be insured. Moreover, it is your responsibility as a buyer to ensure that the goods are insured, and that if the vendor does this then the benefits of the insurance can be passed on to you.

Cargo insurance can be a complicated subject, so you would be well advised to use the services of a broker to advise on and handle the insurance of your goods for you. If you insure at Lloyd's of London you must use a Lloyd's broker, but even though it is not obligatory to use one to deal with an insurance company, it is still advisable.

The main points you must decide are:

1. *The risks against which you wish to insure the goods.* These are now codified by the London Institute of Underwriters who have produced Institute Cargo Clauses A, B and C. A is the nearest to 'All Risks' that you can get although not every risk can be covered. For instance, you cannot insure any illegal transaction (such as importing drugs without a licence), nor can you insure against inherent vice (something inherent in the product which you cannot prevent happening, such as sugar or salt going hard when exposed to water). You have to add a special *war* risk, or a special *strikes* risk if you wish these risks to be included. In fact, you can add almost any risk you like to these Institute clauses. You may care to note that included in these clauses is insurance against what is called *general average*, which you might have to pay if there were any damage to the ship or any of the cargo, caused by any deliberate sacrifice to save the ship from foundering, being lost or damaged. As all the cargo owners would be involved you would be liable, even if you had not insured your goods at all, because any loss falls on all

cargo owners with cargo in that ship, whether damaged or not.

2. *The duration of the insurance.* Under cargo insurance rules the insurance will last from the time the goods leave the supplier's warehouse until they reach the buyer's warehouse. If they come by sea the goods are covered by insurance for 60 days after discharge from the vessel, or on their arrival with you, whichever is the shorter time. By air the period allowed is 30 days. Therefore you must always examine goods as soon as they reach you from abroad to see if they have been damaged or not, or whether any of the consignment is missing.

3. It is up to you, as the buyer, to say for what value the goods are to be insured, or what is called their insured value. It is customary for goods to be insured for their CIF value plus 10 per cent because this will, in the event of a total loss, put you back in the same position as you were before the loss or damage occurred. That is, you receive the full value of the goods you bought plus the freight you will have paid, plus the insurance premium, and an additional 10 per cent of the total to recompense you for being without the goods, and having to wait for their replacement.

4. The premiums you have to pay will depend on many factors, and you must decide the risks against which you insure the goods because the more there are of these risks the higher the premium. But the better the packing of the goods the lower the premium. The longer the time they are in transit the more you pay, so shipments by air tend to pay less insurance than those by sea. Your broker will advise you on these vital points, and he will also shop around the underwriters at Lloyd's, or the insurance companies, to obtain the best cover at the lowest rates. Regular importers or exporters often take out some form of open cover, whereby all shipments are automatically covered by the underwriters, being declared to them after they have been shipped. Premiums are payable monthly, and the great advantage of this open cover is that the importer or exporter can issue his own insurance certificates without waiting for a policy to be prepared, and thus make a claim as soon as the loss or damage is found. Such open cover, and there are several forms it can take, needs a great deal of careful

negotiation when it is essential to use a broker, but it can last indefinitely so is worth taking pains to arrange. The services of the broker are, of course, free to you, since he will be paid by the underwriters.

As an importer you will probably have to make the claim for loss or damage, whoever arranged the insurance, because you are most likely to discover either that some or all of the goods have been damaged, or that some or all of them have been lost. Note here that the interest in the insurance can be passed from the supplier, who arranges the insurance, on to you when you become the owner of the goods, and if you sold them to another importer while they were in transit you could pass on the interest in the insurance to him. Anyone who owns or has a part in handling them has an interest because that person may suffer if there is any loss or damage to the goods. This principle of *insurable interest* is one of the three main principles of insurance, the others being *indemnity* (which means in effect that you will be paid in money, that you cannot be paid twice for the same loss, and that you should recover all the loss), and *utmost good faith* (which means that you must declare to your underwriters all material facts as you know them about the shipment, but that you must presume underwriters know the risks they are taking; if you do not act with UGF your policy will be null and void). These three principles of insurance are contained, along with other provisions, in the Marine Insurance Acts of 1906 and 1909.

As soon as you find that the goods you have bought from overseas have suffered any loss or damage, or even if they fail to arrive altogether, you must call in the Lloyd's or insurance company's agent, to prepare a *survey report*, which certifies the extent of the loss or damage. You must send this survey report to the agent, along with:

1. Evidence that the goods are yours, ie the invoice for them which the supplier will have sent you.
2. Evidence of the shipment of the goods, ie the bill of lading in the case of shipments by sea, the air waybill for shipments by air, the CIM for shipments by rail, or the CMR for shipments by road (see next chapter).
3. Evidence of the insurance of the goods which will be the policy or, as explained above, the certificate of insurance.
4. Copies of letters you will have written to all those likely to have caused the damage or loss, such as the carriers,

those who handled the goods at the port etc. (You need to send out these letters as soon as you have the loss or damage confirmed, and they will be used by your underwriters to recover some of the indemnity they pay to you.)

If you act promptly and within the stipulated times you should have no trouble with your claim and it will be paid in full, including the return of the cost of the survey report (which will not, however, be returned if the claim is refused). But you will appreciate that the loss or damage must have been caused by one of the risks against which the goods have been insured, and in the event of damage you will be paid according to their value on arrival in a damaged condition. You will not, however, lose so you run no risk with cargo insurance of buying goods from overseas and being out of pocket through no fault of your own.

If you are clear in making requests for quotations, equally clear when you place the orders and conclude contracts with your suppliers, and then pay according to the terms agreed, you should have no legal problems over repudiated, broken or frustrated contracts. But you are dealing with people of different nationalities, so make extra sure that everything is clearly understood between you both. As we have said, never make assumptions but always have it spelt out clearly.

Importing is not difficult if you take pains, in the initial stages above all, and having got that right then the rest is fairly simple. We still, however, have to consider transport and documentation problems, and how you will need to pay for the goods, both of these factors affecting the ultimate cost to you of the goods, and these we will cover in the next two chapters.

Chapter 3

Transportation

Having chosen your goods and the supplier from whom you will buy them, you must then decide when and how much to buy, and how you will pay for the goods, because these factors help to determine the eventual price you pay, or the cost to you of the goods. In Chapter 2 it was shown how the price quoted will vary according to the degree of the transport function undertaken by you or your supplier. Moreover, although you, as a buyer, ultimately pay all the costs, it may be that by handling some or all the transport yourself you can effect savings in the cost of the goods because all transport methods do not cost the same. Also, the quantities you import at one time may affect these transport costs, just as they will affect your stock costs.

The Terms of Delivery on which you buy determine the extent of the work you will do in transporting the goods, compared with leaving it to the supplier. If you buy on franco terms you expect to do virtually nothing except pay the customs duty and VAT. If you buy on ex-works terms you would have to do it all. Most importers tend to prefer FOB terms because this gives them the option of either having the suppliers handle the transport (and charging them for so doing), or handling most of it themselves, and in particular of being able to nominate the method of transport, and arranging the insurance themselves. Therefore, as a buyer of goods from overseas, you need some knowledge of international transport, since you may have to deal with it, or at least instruct other people to deal with it for you, apart from instructing your supplier how the goods are to be sent to you.

Handling transport

If you leave the handling of the transport of the goods to your supplier, for example by accepting the goods on CIF terms, you will have to accept his estimate of the costs, and also the efficiency of the transport arrangements he makes. Many buyers dislike CIF for this reason arguing, often quite rightly, that the supplier will have added a margin on his costs to allow for possible increases in freight or insurance costs, and thus will have protected his price. Even if you do accept CIF you will still have to arrange for the goods to be unloaded from the ship or aircraft, cleared through customs and transported to your own warehouse. If you buy on FOB terms you will have to arrange for the transport and for the goods to be insured, all in your supplier's country.

For these functions you will need to use the services of a freight forwarder, and you will be glad to know that most freight forwarders in the UK have agents overseas who can handle this work for you, as well as undertake the work in the UK when the goods arrive.

It is possible for a large company to do this work itself, but as a small business you will almost certainly find it more cost effective to subcontract it to an outside company. Moreover, many freight forwarders operate various forms of transport themselves, and can group shipments for the same destination to different buyers (called groupage) which means a saving in transport costs and some expenses in documents. Freight forwarders charge a percentage of the total freight costs, but they offer their expertise and advice as well as carrying out the work, and you would be well advised to use their services. The Institute of Freight Forwarders can advise on the names of suitable forwarders, some operating worldwide and some specialising in certain types of goods or various parts of the world. You will, of course, have to brief the forwarder so you need to know something about transport and the documents used, and you also need to know how the work should be done to check if he is efficient and if his charges are reasonable. But choosing one is no more or less difficult than choosing any supplier to work for you.

Whether the goods are transported to you as efficiently and cheaply as possible will depend, if you use a freight forwarder, on how well he does his job. In recent surveys some freight forwarders have been shown to be not very efficient, but some of this may be due in part to the inadequate briefing given them by their clients. When you buy services, as when you buy goods, it is up to you not only to choose a good supplier, but also to get the best out of him. This means being clear what transport you wish him to handle, keeping him fully in your confidence, and being yourself sufficiently knowledgeable about transport to be able to do this.

Methods of transport

Your first task will be to decide how the goods are to be sent to you. There are several ways — by sea, air, rail, road or post. It is up to you to decide which will be the most cost effective in your case.

Sea. Most international trade goes by sea because, while it is slow, it is cheap. High volume and low value goods like oil or grain obviously benefit, as does cargo of all weights, shapes and sizes, particularly cargo which can be packed in containers and carried on container ships. Most shipping lines are members of a conference, which guarantees a regular service between two sea ports, and where the charges are always the same whichever line you use. Provided you are not in a hurry for the goods, and can buy in reasonably large quantities — since there is a minimum freight rate — then shipping by sea is probably the best, especially because of its low cost. This is why three-quarters of all goods in the world are moved by sea. It may not, however, always be best for the small importer.

Air. Transporting goods by air is quick but comparatively costly. Where speed is essential, as with goods like flowers or fruit, essential medical supplies, fashion goods etc, then to be able to get goods from virtually anywhere in the world to Britain in 24 hours is worth the additional cost compared with sea transport. An essential spare part or replacement will go by air. A small business may well be able to afford air transport, where the minimum cost is less than by sea, so smaller quantities can be ordered at a time. Most suppliers are near an airport, although not all are near a sea port. It is true airports get congested, but so do sea ports. Air now claims some 25 per cent of all international trade.

Road. Those of you buying from Europe and the Middle East may find that having the goods sent by road, and thus having them delivered to your door, is what you really need. Road transport is cheaper than air, and as the competition for traffic in Europe is intense, rates are highly competitive. It is fairly slow, since there are strict limitations on the number of hours a truck may be driven, while roads in the summer get heavily congested, with long delays at the frontiers. Many freight forwarders have their own road transport services, and will group shipments to a single destination, using containers if necessary. Refrigerated trucks are available as are special trucks for a variety of bulk goods. Roll on/roll off ferries have made delivery by truck relatively easy anywhere in Europe and it may well suit many small businesses who buy on the continent.

Rail. While not many small companies are likely to use rail services from Europe and the Middle East, the railway companies are now introducing a whole variety of specially designed services, which guarantee arrival dates and which are often quicker than the road services. There are container services and, as railways are on the move 24 hours a day and do not have such severe traffic jams, rail transport often has the edge on road.

Post. For many small companies, especially those who buy in small quantities and at frequent intervals, and who do not wish to be bothered with transport problems associated with sea or air, why not use the post? Leave it to the post office to do all the work, and your sole problem is that only small quantities at a time can be sent in one parcel, although you can have as many parcels sent as you wish. The post office offers a number of services: there is the ordinary parcel post, by air or sea; a letter post for small packets or the printed paper post. Moreover, all that has to be done is for the parcel to be handed in at a post office by your supplier, and it will be delivered direct to you. In addition, the postman will collect customs and VAT charges on small value consignments up to £25, and also on those valued up to £50 provided you complete a declaration of value and content. It is only for goods valued over £50 that you have to use more forms, as shown in Chapter 5.

In fact it is difficult to beat the post office for speed and ease of documentation. Provided the goods you are buying are small and light enough to be sent in a parcel, for many small businesses some form of post might be the best answer because of the international network of postal services which has been developed over the years, using sea, air, rail and road services.

Costs of transport

In addition to deciding on the method of transport for your goods you must take into account the costs of each method, and to do this you must know how the various services charge their freight.

When you despatch by sea the shipping lines will charge you the rate applicable to your type of goods to London, or other UK ports, from the supplier's port, and they will calculate their charges on a weight/volume basis. That is to say, they will wish to know the size of the consignment, which you must measure in cubic centimetres, and then turn into cubic metres — by dividing by 1 million. They will also ask for the weight, which you will obtain in kilograms, and then turn into metric tonnes — by dividing by 1000. Whichever is the greater figure will be the one used to calculate what you pay in freight charges plus, of course, any surcharges which may be in force, such as for port congestion, extra fuel costs etc. For example, if your consignment measures 2.5 cubic metres and weighs 1.7 metric tonnes, you will be charged 2½ times the freight rate. On this ratio remember that most consignments will be charged on a measurement rather than a weight basis. If you use conference line ships the basic rate will be the same on all conference vessels, less any discounts for the regular use of a certain line. There are a variety of rates depending on the type of goods, length of voyage etc, and these will be quoted by the shipping lines. Freight is normally payable in advance, a service a freight forwarder will provide for you.

When you ship by road or rail the same weight/volume ratios will apply. Rail rates are standard throughout Europe, but road rates are highly competitive, and have to be negotiated with the carriers, who will base their rates on a number of factors, such as whether they have return loads etc.

When you ship by air the rates will be the same for all IATA airlines, and will depend on length of voyage, type of commodity etc. But while the airlines also use a weight/volume ratio, in their case it is 7000 cubic centimetres to one kilogram. (This is the IATA — International Air Transport Association — rate; non-IATA lines have different rates.) On this basis most goods sent by air pay by weight, as you might expect, since weight is the most important factor in air freight.

Postal rates are based on weight and vary according to the type of service and destination. These rates are all shown in the *Post Office Guide*, and there is a maximum weight allowed of 20 kilograms from most destinations overseas. Rates include door-to-door delivery and, as you have seen, in some cases the collection of customs duty and payment of VAT will also be done by the post office.

As a customer you must decide how you wish the goods to be sent to you by your suppliers, and you must weigh up the respective methods and costs of each, before either instructing your suppliers or having the transport arranged by a freight forwarder, or even handling it yourself. The factors you must consider are:

1. *The type of goods you are importing*, for instance heavy goods not urgently required are best sent by sea, whereas perishable goods, such as flowers or fruit which are fairly light in weight, go by air, as do goods you require very quickly. Small consignments can well be sent by post, while goods requiring door-to-door delivery to you from Europe go best by road, especially if your supplier has his own road transport or regularly delivers by road to the UK.

2. *The quantities you order at one time*, because there are minimum rates by sea and air, and in both cases the cost of documentation will be the same whatever the quantities involved. Sea, rail and road tend to favour larger quantities, with air and post perhaps better for smaller quantities at a time.

3. *The urgency of the transport*, that is to say how far in advance you can order, or how essential a quick delivery date is to you.

4. *The costs involved.* For example, is it worth paying extra for air freight; will the quicker delivery enable you to sell the goods you have imported more quickly and thus obtain a quicker return on your money?

A great deal will depend on previous experience, so you should not only try different methods of transport but also compare their cost effectiveness. Take the advice of your suppliers, who should be knowledgeable about transport and who will wish to see that you are a satisfied customer.

There is one other factor which may affect the way goods are sent to you, and this is how your supplier expects you to pay for them. This is because, excepting despatches by sea, the goods will be delivered to you, or you can collect them, irrespective of whether you have paid for them or not. If, however, your supplier insists on being paid before you take possession of the goods, he would probably insist on shipment by sea, and you would have to agree. He can therefore withhold the documents you need to gain possession until payment is made, if the goods are sent by sea. This will be made clear later in this chapter and in the next.

Packing and marking of goods

While you would normally leave it to your supplier to pack

the goods for shipment properly, you must be careful to specify any special packing you may feel is necessary to protect them from loss or damage, since you will be the loser if they are inadequately packed. Packing will vary according to the type of goods you buy and you will probably have considerable experience of this. It will also vary according to the method of transport used, and you may feel that sending goods, say, by air will save money on packing or prevent their being damaged as easily as if they were sent by sea. The cost of extra packing should be queried, and while packing is normally included in the price, you should make sure that there will be no extra costs involved or, if there are, what these will be.

The two major developments in packing have been, first, the introduction of pallets, where several consignments are loaded on to a wooden or steel pallet and shipped as one consignment. This reduces handling costs and lessens the danger of any of the goods being lost.

The second major development has been the introduction of containers, the goods being transported in standard-sized wooden or steel boxes. This type of shipment is most suitable for small goods of all kinds, since it reduces the danger of their being stolen, mislaid or damaged, while it also means that they are at less risk during handling at sea or airports. Containers can be carried by sea, air, road or rail, and the total cost of shipment is often less for goods sent in containers than as separate packages. You can ask your supplier to ship in a container. If you order a sufficient quantity then your supplier can ship a full container load (FCL), and that container will be delivered to you to unpack as you wish. If the quantity is insufficient for a full container load, the goods can still share a container with goods of other customers, when they will be unloaded at a container depot in the UK, and then delivered to the various customers. However, remember that goods still need some packing if they are transported in this way, because containers can sweat, while goods can rattle round in the container and get damaged unless adequately protected. Your insurance costs will probably be less on goods shipped in containers, and you will find, moreover, that many shipping lines run far more container ships than conventional cargo ships. Airlines, as well as rail and road services, are all concentrating on shipments by container because of their greater ease of handling.

Marking

In addition to being clear on how your imports have to be packed, you must also instruct your suppliers how they are to be marked. There is today a fairly standard set of markings for goods sent by sea, and you should ask your supplier to mark the consignment with:

1. The order number of the consignment, preferably your own number, so when the goods arrive you know to which order they belong.
2. The destination, that is, the port to which the goods are coming, eg Southampton or Liverpool. If the goods are coming on to you in, say, Birmingham, and are being sent by the port of Felixstowe, then the goods should be marked 'Birmingham via Felixstowe'.
3. Where the consignment consists of several packages they will need to be numbered, and this is done by using the second number shown to indicate the total number of packages, and the first number to show which package it is. So with 4 packages you would have the first numbered 1/4, then 2/4 and 3/4, so that 4/4 means the fourth package in a consignment of four.
4. The mark you wish to have used so that you may identify the goods as yours when they arrive at a port. Normally companies use their initials, sometimes put in a distinctive shape. You could have them marked SM and put a circle round the two letters.

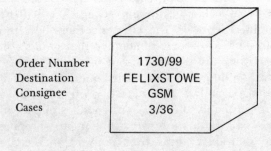

Order Number   1730/99
Destination   FELIXSTOWE
Consignee   GSM
Cases   3/36

Figure 3.1 *Case markings*

When goods are sent by air, road, rail or post they can be addressed to you in the normal way because they will be delivered to your address.

Never have the contents shown on a package as this is an invitation to thieves. If you wish to identify what is in a number of packages in the same consignment, ask your supplier to include a *packing list* with the documents he sends you.

You will need to instruct your supplier clearly on these points, since he must not only pack to your instructions but he will also need all this information when he fills in or raises the shipping documents, just as you will need it for your import documents. The weights and measurements of the consignment will also have to be shown on the documents.

There are other marks in fairly general use, such as an upright wine glass for 'this side up', or a broken wine glass for fragile goods, and special marks for dangerous or flammable goods, but your supplier will be well aware of these.

Good packing will help to reduce the risks of loss or damage, while efficient marking will enable you to pick the goods out when they arrive, and examine them quickly to ensure they are all present and correct, or make your claim on the insurance underwriters if anything is wrong. Do not rely on your supplier to do all this, but make it clear to him that you need them packed and marked as suits you, and explain exactly what you want. These instructions will, of course, be part of the order you send.

Shipping documents

When goods are sent by sea, the shipping line will issue to the shipper a document known as a *Bill of Lading*, and you as the importer will need this document when you go to collect the goods, so it is essential that you are familiar with its uses. If you or your freight forwarder are arranging the shipment by sea you will be given the bill of lading, or B/L.

A conventional bill of lading has three main functions:

1. It is a contract of carriage between the shipping line and the consignor of the goods, and it states clearly the conditions under which the shipping line will carry those goods, and for what it is responsible. The conditions are numerous and detailed, but all you really need to know is that, provided the consignor carries out his side of the

EASTERN TRADING Ltd

P O Box 500, MARINE PARADE POST OFFICE, SINGAPORE 9144
REPUBLIC OF SINGAPORE

PACKING LIST

ORDER NO. 634781

COUNTRY OF DESTINATION: United Kingdom

VESSEL/AIRCRAFT ETC: "Silver Crown"

INVOICE TO:

Kasha Importers Ltd
49 New Street
Bedlington
Essex
United Kingdom

MARKS AND NUMBERS	DESCRIPTION	MEASUREMENT (cms)	WEIGHT (Kilos) Gross	Net
KIL Dover Nos. 1 - 24	Leather belts and straps	85x85x100	9.3	8.1
KIL Dover Nos. 25 - 36	Leather handbags (440 pieces)	110x85x100	9.5	8.5

Gross Weight: 337.2 Kilos.

Net Weight: 296.4 Kilos.

DATE: 18.6.198..

SIGNATURE:

Figure 3.2 *Packing list*

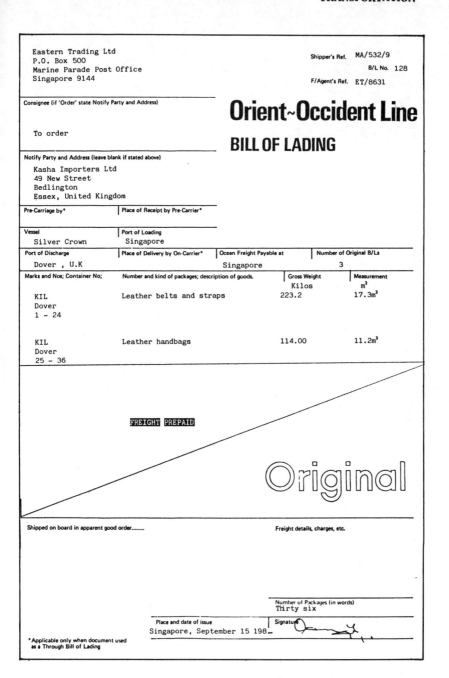

Figure 3.3 *Bill of lading*

COMPANHIA PORTUGUESA DE TRANSPORTES MARÍTIMOS, E.P.

RUA DE S. JULIÃO, 63 — 1116 LISBOA CODEX
APARTADO 2747 — TELEF. 36 96 21/9 — TELEX 12440 CTMLX P

TRAFFIC LINE: Chamcom

ORIGINAL
B/L
N.º 85621
ATTENTION
This B/L is not valid for clearance before validated by the ship's Agent

Vessel Silver Streak	Port of loading: Lisbon	Port of destination Liverpool

Shipper	Consigned to order of
Juarez Rua Sa do Bandeiro 27 3400 Lisbon	Shipper

Clearing Agent	Notify address*
Acme Forwarders 12 Highlove Road Liverpool	Kasha Importers Ltd 49 New Street Bedlington, Essex. U.K. * (Without any responsability of notification by Shipowners, other carriers and / or their Agents respectively, if shippers or consignees fail in their obligations).

Freight payable at: Liverpool

Number of original Ba/L 3

Marks	Nos.	Quantity	Kind of packages	Description of goods	Measurement cbm		Gross weight kos.
KIL LIV	1 - 10	10	Cases	Assorted footwear	17	500	881

PARTICULARS FURNISHED BY SHIPPERS OF GOODS.

Freight and Charges

$3,570.

SHIPPED on board in apparent good order and condition, weight, measure, marks, numbers, quality, contents and value unknown, for carriage to the port of discharge or so near thereunto as the vessel may safely get and lie always afloat, to be delivered in the like good order and condition at the aforesaid port unto Consignees or their Assignees, they paying freight as per note on the margin plus other charges incurred in accordance with the provisions contained in this Bill of Lading.

In accepting this Bill of Lading the Merchant expressly accepts and agrees to all its stipulations on both pages, whether written, printed, stamped or otherwise incorporated, as fully as if they were all signed by the Merchant. One original Bill of Lading must be surrendered duly endorsed in exchange for the goods or delivery order.

IN WITNESS whereof the Master of the said Vessel has signed the number of original Bills of Lading stated above, all of his tenor and date, one of which being accomplished the others to stand void.

Place and date of issue

Lisbon 17.7.198..

The Shipper

Signed (for the master) by

Mod. 172 - Ref. 7163

Figure 3.4 *Bill of lading*

contract and pays the freight, the shipping line will take the goods to, say, the UK port named in the bill of lading or as near to that port as the ship may safely proceed without endangering the ship or its cargo. They do not guarantee the goods will arrive at any stated time, but they will endeavour to arrive on schedule and, moreover, with the consignment in good condition.

2. As the bill of lading acts as a receipt for the goods, the shipping line qualify this receipt with the words, 'Received or shipped in apparent good order and condition', which means they agree the goods are in their possession and appear to be as described on the B/L. Should the goods appear to be damaged, or some are missing, they will 'clause' the B/L, indicating that the goods are not as described on the B/L. This is known as a dirty B/L.

3. The bill of lading also acts as a document of title to the goods, which is quasi-negotiable. This means in effect that the title can be passed on from, say, the shipper to the customer by endorsing it accordingly.

In addition it is a condition of the shipping line that the original bill of lading (bills are issued in sets of originals and copies) must be surrendered to the shipping line before the goods will be handed over to the consignee. If you have paid for the goods your supplier — if he is doing the shipping — or your freight forwarder will need to send you the original bills of lading to enable you to lodge one of them with the shipping line in the UK, and thus obtain a delivery order from them. If, however, the supplier wishes to obtain payment from you, or a promise to pay, by means of a bill of exchange; or if you are paying by documentary letter of credit and you wish to ensure the supplier is not paid until the documents of title to the goods are on their way to you, then the bill of lading may be withheld until you pay or agree to pay; or your supplier will not be paid locally unless your bank has those bills of lading (see Chapter 4 for details of these transactions).

Should by any chance the goods arrive and the bills of lading are not with you, as frequently happens today, they become known as *stale bills*, and your only way of getting the goods is to give the shipping line a bank letter of indemnity. If the goods arrive and have to be stored by the shipping line you will be charged demurrage, ie the cost of that storage.

Those are the essential features of a conventional bill of

lading and what you as the consignee need is a complete set of clean, original bills of lading, showing that the goods are as you have ordered and are in good condition.

Note that a bill of lading will usually be marked 'freight paid' because shipping lines prefer freight to be paid in advance, although arrangements can be made for you to pay the freight on arrival, when the bills will be so marked.

There are other types of bills of lading, such as a *short form bill of lading*, which is the same as a conventional one except that the conditions of carriage are not shown on the back. A *sea waybill* is different in that it is not a document of title, so does not have to be produced for the shipping line to obtain delivery of the goods. In these days of fast sea transport there is an increasing use of sea waybills, provided the consignor does not wish to withhold delivery to the consignee until payment is made. A *container bill* is more or less the same as a conventional bill provided it is for a full container load, but where goods are sent to you as part of other goods in a container, then the container line will issue you with a *house bill*, which you surrender to them at the depot when you go to collect the goods.

There is a great deal more to bills of lading than this, but as a small business you may not become greatly involved if you do not have many shipments by sea. At least you will know the essentials, and this is by far the most complicated of the shipping documents.

When shipping by air the consignor will be given an *air waybill* by the airline. It acts as a receipt for the goods and a contract of carriage, but the goods must be delivered to you as the consignee, and it is not a document of title. You will probably receive it after the goods have been shipped, as the consignee's copy normally accompanies the goods on the aircraft. All you need to know is the number of the AWB, as when you take delivery you will usually find the goods are stored and then identified by their air waybill number, along with the identity of the first carrier. So make sure your supplier telexes or phones you with the air waybill number, or you may have difficulty when you go to the airport to collect your goods. After all, there is no point in paying extra for shipments by air if time is wasted on the ground.

For goods sent by road the carrier issues a document which is the equivalent of the air waybill, namely a *CMR note*, but this is mainly for the carrier's use. You do not need it to obtain

STRATEGIC EUROPEAN LINE **BILL OF LADING** FOR COMBINED TRANSPORT AND PORT TO PORT SHIPMENT

SHIPPER/EXPORTER (2) (COMPLETE NAME AND ADDRESS)

DOCUMENT NO. (5)

EXPORT REFERENCES (6)

CONSIGNEE (3) (COMPLETE NAME AND ADDRESS)

FORWARDING AGENT — REFERENCES (7) (COMPLETE NAME AND ADDRESS)

POINT AND COUNTRY OF ORIGIN (8)

NOTIFY PARTY (4) (COMPLETE NAME AND ADDRESS)

FOR DELIVERY APPLY TO: (9)

PIER/TERMINAL (10)

VESSEL (11) FLAG PORT OF LOADING (12) ONWARD INLAND ROUTING (15)

PORT OF DISCHARGE FROM VESSEL (13) FOR TRANSSHIPMENT TO (14)

PARTICULARS FURNISHED BY SHIPPER				
MARKS AND NUMBERS (16)	NO. OF PKGS. (17)	DESCRIPTION OF PACKAGES AND GOODS (18)	GROSS WEIGHT (19)	MEASUREMENT (20)

PREPAID COLLECT

RECEIVED the goods or containers, vans, trailers, pallet units or other packages said to contain goods herein mentioned, in apparent good order and condition, except as otherwise indicated, to be transported, delivered or transshipped as provided herein. All of the provisions written, printed or stamped on either side hereof are part of this bill of lading contract.

IN WITNESS WHEREOF, the Carrier by its agent has signed ___THREE___ bills of lading, all of the same tenor and date, one of which being accomplished, the others to stand void.

TOTAL OCEAN FREIGHT CHARGES

CHARGES OTHER THAN OCEAN TRANSPORTATION

CHARGES ADVANCED

BY _____

TOTAL

FOR CARRIER

DATED B/L NO.

STC-102/3 REV. 8/82 STC B/L

Figure 3.5(a) *Combined transport bill of lading — used for containers etc*

SHORT FORM BILL OF LADING
(Terms continued from overside)

If this Bill of Lading evidences a contract for the carriage of goods by sea to or from ports of the United States, in foreign trade, or provides for routing within the United States, it shall have effect subject to the provisions of the U.S. Carriage of Goods by Sea Act of 1936, and other applicable statutes, to the extent that any such Act or Statute may apply to the transportation contract of any one or more of the carriers involved.

As used herein, the term "Carrier" means Strategic Transportation Company, Inc. and all other Carriers whether on land or sea on whose modes of conveyance the goods described on the face hereof are carried.

The Carrier's regular long form Bill of Lading may contain a number of provisions giving the Carrier certain rights and privileges and certain exceptions and immunities from and limitations of liability additional to those provided by the Acts or Laws referred to above and may extend the benefit of its provisions to stevedores and others.

All agreements with respect to the above goods are superseded hereby and none of the terms hereof shall be deemed waived except in writing by an authorized Agent of the Carrier.

This short form Bill of Lading is provided by the Shipper and issued for his convenience and at his request instead of the Carrier's regular long form Bill of Lading. Copies of the Carrier's regular long form Bill of Lading and the clauses presently being stamped or endorsed thereon are available from the Carrier on request and are incorporated in tariffs or classifications on file with the Interstate Commerce Commission or the Federal Maritime Commission.

In using this short form Bill of Lading, the Shipper, Consignee, and Holder hereof agree that all the terms and conditions of the Carrier's regular long form Bill of Lading, normally used in the service for which this Bill of Lading is issued, including any clauses presently being stamped or endorsed thereon filed with the above agencies, are incorporated herein with like force and effect as if they were written at length herein, and all such terms and conditions so incorporated by reference are agreed by Shipper to be binding and to govern the relations, whatever they may be, between all who are or may become parties to this Bill of Lading as fully as if this Bill of Lading had been prepared on the Carrier's regular long form Bill of Lading.

If required by the Carrier, a signed original Bill of Lading, duly endorsed, must be surrendered to the Carrier or its Agent before delivery of the goods.

The liability of the Carrier as to the value of shipment at the rate herein provided shall be determined in accordance with the clauses of the Carrier's regular Bill of Lading form. If the Shipper desires to be covered for a valuation in excess of that allowed by the Carrier's regular Bill of Lading form, the Shipper must so stipulate in Carrier's Bill of Lading covering such shipments and such additional liability will be assumed to be the Carrier's only where the Shipper has made such a request and has paid an additional charge in accordance with Rule No. 12 on the total declared valuation, in addition to the stipulated rate on the commodities shipped as specified herein. A Shipper who has elected to show value of goods on the Bill of Lading shall be deemed to have desired to be covered for the value excess of that allowed by the Carrier's regular Bill of Lading form, and must be assessed the above mentioned additional charge. Carrier's liability, irrespective of fault or negligence, will be limited, to $500 per package as delivered or container and contents, and covering Bill of Lading shall contain the following:

"Shipper hereby agrees that Carrier's liability is limited to $500 with respect to the container and entire contents (including container if not supplied by the Carrier), except when Shipper declares a higher valuation and shall have paid additional freight on such declared valuation pursuant to proper rule in this tariff. Notwithstanding any other provision herein, in no event, including negligence, will Carrier be liable for indirect, special or consequential loss or damage."

For the Carrier's complete terms and conditions of carriage, please refer to FMC Tariff Number Three effective September 1, 1982.

WORLD HEADQUARTERS
STRATEGIC TRANSPORTATION COMPANY, INC.
P.O. BOX 52800
HOUSTON, TX 77052
TEL. (713) 680-3775
TELEX: 792240

Figure 3.5(b) *(Combined transport) reverse of short form bill of lading*

AIR WAYBILL NUMBER	NOT NEGOTIABLE AIR WAYBILL AIR CONSIGNMENT NOTE	
140935		140935

Airport of Departure (Address of First Carrier) and Requested Routing
New York

AIRPORT OF DESTINATION
London, Heathrow

ROUTING AND DESTINATION

TO	BY FIRST CARRIER B.A	TO	BY	TO	BY	TO	BY

CONSIGNEE'S ACCOUNT NUMBER | CONSIGNEE'S NAME AND ADDRESS

Kasha Importers Ltd
49 New Street
Bedlington
Essex
United Kingdom

ISSUED BY: BEHRING INTERNATIONAL, INC.
10700 NORTHWEST FREEWAY
HOUSTON, TEXAS 77092

C.A.B. REG. INTERNATIONAL AIR FREIGHT FORWARDERS

CARRIER'S LIMITATION OF LIABILITY AND TIME LIMITS FOR FILING OF CLAIMS ARE GOVERNED BY CONDITIONS OF CONTRACT ON REVERSE SIDE.

SHIPPER'S ACCOUNT NUMBER | SHIPPER'S NAME AND ADDRESS

The shipper certifies that the particulars on the face hereof are correct and agrees to the CONDITIONS ON REVERSE HEREOF.

SIGNATURE OF SHIPPER

M.B. Joseph Co. Inc.
196 - 15B 65th Street
New York, NY 98246
U.S.A.

BY BROKER/AGENT

Carrier certifies goods described below were received for carriage subject to the CONDITIONS ON REVERSE HEREOF, the goods then being in apparent good order and condition except as noted hereon.

SHIPPER'S REF. NO.

ISSUING CARRIER'S AGENT, ACCOUNT NO. | ISSUING CARRIER'S AGENT, NAME AND CITY

EXECUTED ON 8.8.198.. (Date) AT New York (Place)

AGENT'S IATA CODE
119 - 82 - 9056

INSURANCE—If Shipper requests insurance in accordance with conditions on reverse hereof, indicate amount of insurance in figures in box marked 'Amount of Insurance' below.

SIGNATURE OF ISSUING CARRIER OR ITS AGENT

Copies 1, 2 and 3 of this Air Waybill are originals and have the same validity.

CHARGES Prepaid Collect	CURRENCY	DECLARED VALUE FOR CARRIAGE	DECLARED VALUE FOR CUSTOMS	AMOUNT OF INSURANCE	COD AMOUNT	SPECIAL ACCOUNTING INFORMATION
X	US $	NVD	$4,500.00			

No. of Packages RCP	ACTUAL GROSS WEIGHT	Kg./lb	Rate Class	COMMODITY ITEM NO.	CHARGEABLE WEIGHT	RATE	NATURE AND QUANTITY OF GOODS (INCL. DIMENSIONS OR VOLUME)
3	158.8	K	Q		159.0	2.50	Photographic goods
							Dims: 3 @ 36 x 24 x 14 ins.
							THESE COMMODITIES ARE LICENSED BY THE U.S. FOR ULTIMATE DESTINATION. DIVERSION CONTRARY TO U.S. LAW PROHIBITED.

SPECIAL HANDLING INFORMATION (INCLUDING MARKS, NUMBERS AND METHOD OF PACKING)
Three (3) cases   Marks: KIL 4705/1-3

DOCUMENTS TO ACCOMPANY AWB
☐ COMM'L. INV. ☐ CONSULAR INV. ☐ OTHER

PREPAID

WEIGHT CHARGE	VALUATION CHARGE	TOTAL OF AIRLINE CHARGES BELOW	AWB FEE	CODE	TOTAL OF NON-AIRLINE CHARGES BELOW ORIGIN	DESTINATION	COLLECT CHARGES IN DESTINATION CURRENCY
397.50			4.50	(A)			WEIGHT CHARGE

AIRLINE AND NON-AIRLINE CHARGES, OTHER THAN WEIGHT CHARGE, VALUATION CHARGE AND AWB FEE
Handling 27.50

TOTAL PREPAID	AIRLINE AND NON-AIRLINE CHARGES, CONTINUED			VALUATION CHARGE
429.50				

COLLECT

WEIGHT CHARGE	VALUATION CHARGE	TOTAL OF AIRLINE CHARGES BELOW	Agent's Disbursements	TOTAL OF NON-AIRLINE CHARGES BELOW ORIGIN	DESTINATION	Other Charges incl. COD Fee

AIRLINE AND NON-AIRLINE CHARGES, OTHER THAN WEIGHT CHARGE, VALUATION CHARGE AND AGENT'S DISBURSEMENTS

COD

COD AMOUNT	COD FEE	AIRLINE AND NON AIRLINE CHARGES, CONTINUED	TOTAL COLLECT

FOR CARRIER'S USE ONLY AT DESTINATION

BI 400 (REV. 10/81) INT'L HOUSE AIR WAYBILL

ORIGINAL (1) FOR SHIPPER

Figure 3.6 *House air waybill*

delivery, and it serves only as a receipt for the goods and a contract of carriage. The equivalent document for shipments by rail is called a *CIM note*.

When goods are sent to you by post the packages must be accompanied by a properly completed customs declaration, either on Form C2/CP3 or Form C1 (a green label) as appropriate, which describes in full the nature, quantity and value of the goods contained in the package.

Checklist

Since transport and documentation costs will add greatly to the basic price of the goods, you must consider with some care how they can best be sent to you, and so arrange it that:

1. The most appropriate method of transport is used.
2. The costs of the transport are kept to a minimum.
3. The goods are packed so as to avoid any possibility of loss or damage to them in transit.
4. The goods are so marked by the suppliers as to be easily identifiable during their voyage and on arrival in the UK.
5. The documentation for the shipping part of the transaction is correct and so arranged that you can obtain the goods easily on arrival. There are, of course, many other documents concerned with importing goods from overseas, but these will be explained in Chapter 6.
6. All your instructions on these points are clearly stated on the orders you send to your suppliers, because you should not assume they will know what you want them to do; or, if you are doing some or all of the transport yourself, with or without a forwarding agent, that you and he are properly and clearly briefed.

Your supplier will be conversant with these points, and should have experience in dealing with them if he is a regular exporter to the UK. But as the lower the costs of transportation the less the final cost of the goods will be to you, so it is your responsibility in the first place to ensure that transportation is done as efficiently and cheaply as possible.

Before, however, you can arrive at a final cost of the goods to you, you must take into account how you will pay for them.

Chapter 4

Terms and Methods of Payment

Obviously, an exporter wants to be sure, first that you can pay, and second, that you will pay, in full, as quickly as possible.

From your point of view as an importer, the two most important payment factors are first, that your reputation as a paying customer is such that your supplier trusts you; second, that you have as long as possible to pay, because this lowers the actual cost of the goods to you.

Creditworthiness

From the outset, when purchasing from overseas sources you must establish your creditworthiness with your suppliers. They will, if they are competent exporters, be sure to check this before entering into any contracts with you. So when you ask for a quotation, or send out an order, be sure to quote the name of your bank, and invite your supplier to ask for a reference. Your bank will, if you are a good customer, give you a good but guarded reference, but be sure to discuss it with them in advance if it is for an unusually large sum, or one that is larger than you normally use.

In addition you should always be meticulous about paying overseas suppliers on the due date, so that when they check you out you will be told that you pay regularly and promptly. Exporters nearly always check among themselves on new customers overseas, and they are astonishingly quick to hear about unreliable customers. The better your creditworthiness the better payment terms you should obtain, and this is all part and parcel of being a good importer.

Methods of payment

There are several ways by which you can pay for goods bought from overseas. You have to decide which suits you best, although this will also depend to some degree on what terms your supplier will demand, so it is really a matter for mutual negotiation.

We propose to examine seven methods of payment, five of which are commonly used in the import/export trade.

1. Cash in advance

From a supplier's point of view this is probably the most advantageous method of payment, because the buyer pays for the goods in full before they are sent to him. From your point of view it is probably the least satisfactory, because having paid, you are not sure the supplier will ever send the goods. Moreover, you are out of your money from the time you send it until you receive the goods, which could be from six to nine months.

Exporters do sometimes insist on cash in advance, especially from customers in countries they do not know, or of whose ability to pay they have doubts; hence the importance of establishing your creditworthiness. (An exporter is taught always to have an order checked by his own credit control before he accepts it.)

Where long-term contracts are involved part payment may be demanded in advance, with the remainder in instalments, but there will generally be safeguards written into the contract, with the banks guaranteeing payment.

If you are forced to pay in advance you can send a cheque, which will take some time to clear. You can send a banker's draft, which might be stolen. Better still you can make use of the computer system called SWIFT, which is used by some banks to transfer money from banks in one country to those in another.

Should your supplier demand cash in advance you could reasonably ask for a sizeable discount, equal to the cost of the money during the time you do not have its use. Even a deposit is not really satisfactory for either side, because if you pay, say, 50 per cent in advance and the balance after you receive the goods, your supplier is never sure that you will actually pay the other 50 per cent, while you might doubt, having paid 50 per cent, whether you would in fact receive the goods.

On the whole, therefore, we do not recommend this method of payment, because most of the advantages are with the supplier, and if you are a good customer, with a good credit rating, you should be able to obtain better terms.

2. Documentary letter of credit

A great deal of import/export business is done on the basis of payment by means of a documentary letter of credit, because this gives both you and your supplier some protection. The system works as follows:

As a buyer you open a documentary letter of credit through your own bank, in favour of your supplier overseas. It clearly states how much you are prepared to pay, and when and under what conditions you will pay. You know, therefore, to what you are committed, and your supplier knows that if he fulfils the conditions you lay down, he will get paid.

Normally the conditions you would write into a documentary letter of credit would be:

(a) The goods you wish to be sent, their price, packing etc.
(b) The total amount of the credit, ie the price you are paying plus any other amounts such as for transport, insurance etc.
(c) The latest date of despatch of the goods and the method of transport to be used.
(d) The latest date on which the credit will be paid, usually taken to be some four to six weeks after the latest date of shipment.
(e) The documents you require to be sent to you. In the case of shipment by sea this must include the bill of lading, to enable you to obtain delivery of the goods. Copies of the shipping documents are sufficient in the case of other transport methods. In all cases you will require other documents, which will be dealt with in Chapter 6. All the documents you need, with their number of copies, must be clearly set down.
(f) Any other conditions you care to impose, such as no part shipments, no transhipment, no shipment by a certain carrier etc. You may lay down any conditions you care to include, but these are the most common.

You then instruct your bank to open this credit in favour of your supplier, and you ask the bank to ensure that the credit is:

(a) Irrevocable, which means it cannot be altered without the agreement of your supplier and yourself.
(b) Confirmed. This means your UK bank will ask a bank in the supplier's country to confirm payment to the supplier, your bank sending them the credit to enable this to be done.
(c) Subject to the 'Uniform Customs and Practice for Documentary Credits' (No 400, 1983, of the International

INTERNATIONAL BANK plc
15 High Street, London EC31B 5AL
Tel. 01 966 53821   Telex: 13611898

DOCUMENTARY CREDIT NO. LCC/697/A   Date 30 June 198..

Beneficiary: Eastern Trading Ltd,   Advising Bank:
              P.O. Box 500   International Bank plc
              Marine Parade Post Office   Coleman Way
              Singapore 9144   Singapore 8367

Dear Sirs,

We have opened the above irrevocable credit in your favour up to the amount of
£6,255.00 (say six thousand, two hundred and fifty five pounds sterling) valid
until 30 September 198..   By order of Kasha Importers Ltd.

This is available against the following documents:

1. Commercial invoice in triplicate showing name of the manufacturer or producer
   of the goods.
2. Packing list in triplicate.
3. Full set, clean on board negotiable Bills of Lading to the order of the
   shipper, marked freight prepaid and blank endorsed dated not later than
   September 18, 198..
4. Form A (APR) countersigned by the Chamber of Commerce.

Covering: 560 Leather belts (assorted)

              500 Leather straps (luggage)

              440 Leather handbags (assorted)

All as Pro-forma invoice A/634781

Insurance to be effected by Kasha Importers Ltd

Delivery C & F U.K. Port
Partial Shipments   permitted
Transhipments   permitted

Documents to be presented within 21 days after the date of issuance of the
shipping document(s) but within the validity of the credit.

All drafts drawn under this Credit must contain the clause "Drawn under D/C No.
LCC/697/A" and we undertake to honour such drafts on presentation provided they
ARE DRAWN AND PRESENTED IN conformity with the terms of this credit.

Except as otherwise expressly stated this credit is subject to Uniform Customs
and Practice for Documentary Credits International Chamber of Commerce Brochure
No. 400.

                                Yours faithfully
                                For International Bank plc

                                Manager

Figure 4.1 *Documentary credit*

Chamber of Commerce) which came into force in 1984. This sets out all the rules which the ICC have agreed for the handling of documentary credits, and under which any disagreements would be resolved.

Having asked your bank to open such a credit, you must satisfy them that you have sufficient money for it to be paid when due. You will, therefore, have to space out such credits, when you open them, according to your cash flow, but you will be accustomed to doing this exercise with your normal domestic purchases.

Your bank will send this credit to a bank they use in the supplier's country, and ask them to advise the supplier they have such a credit in his favour. The supplier will be requested to agree that he accepts the credit as you have worded it. If he does then you will be advised that it is accepted and your supplier will go ahead and ship you the goods. He will send the documents you have requested to the local bank who will send them to you through your bank so you can take delivery of the goods when they arrive. As soon as the supplier sends all the named documents to the bank in his country, and the bank are satisfied they are exactly as you requested, the supplier will be paid the full amount of the credit.

The supplier has the option of asking you to change some or all of the conditions you have laid down, and it is up to you whether or not you agree. You will have to pay your bank to open the credit, and you would have to pay again to have it altered, so try to get it right the first time. Ask your bank for their advice; banks in the UK are extremely knowledgeable about letters of credit from all over the world.

Notice that the great advantage to you is that you do not pay until the supplier has shipped the goods and prepared and handed over all the necessary documentation, so you know you will receive the goods for which you have paid. Your supplier equally knows that, provided he carries out all the conditions you have laid down, he will be paid. So you both have that degree of protection, which is why so much international trade is paid for by means of documentary letters of credit. On the other hand, you suffer to some degree because you have to guarantee the amount of the credit to the bank so you might not get the goods until some time after you have paid for them; you get no credit from your supplier; and while the banks will check the documents carefully before parting with your money, they will not examine the goods or be responsible for their being exactly as described on the documents. But your supplier would be in serious breach of contract with you if he were not to despatch the goods as shown on the documents.

The above describes a standard documentary letter of credit, but there are several other kinds, of which two may be helpful to you. One is the *revolving credit*, which you can use if you are buying several consignments of goods at regular intervals. You open a revolving credit on exactly the same lines as a documentary letter of credit but with the proviso that as soon as the sum indicated on the credit is used for one shipment, it is automatically renewed for a second shipment, and so on. This saves you the expense of opening a fresh credit for each consignment.

The second is a *transferable credit*, sometimes asked for by a supplier who is not the manufacturer of the goods. By making the credit transferable the supplier can pay the manufacturer a share of the credit, and then be paid his share from the balance, the total being within the amount you are prepared to pay for the goods.

3. Bills of exchange

You may wish to pay after the goods arrive or even later, on the basis that this would give you time to resell them and thus recover some of the money you need to pay out. After all, you are taking the risk that you might not be able to use or resell the goods, so why should all the risks be with you, and not partly at least with the supplier?

At the same time your supplier will wish to be satisfied that if he sends you the goods you will pay for them, since otherwise he would be taking all the risks of non-payment, and possibly never get his money.

A bill of exchange, as you may well know, is a legal document drawn on one person by another, requesting that a certain sum of money be paid for goods or services supplied.

Your supplier, having sent the goods you ordered, will draw a draft on you (a bill of exchange starts as a draft, and becomes a bill after it has been paid or accepted). The supplier sends this draft to his bank with all the shipping documents, and requests his bank to have the draft presented to you by a bank in the UK. This British bank would then present you with the draft and hand over the documents enabling you to take delivery of the goods, provided you paid or accepted that draft.

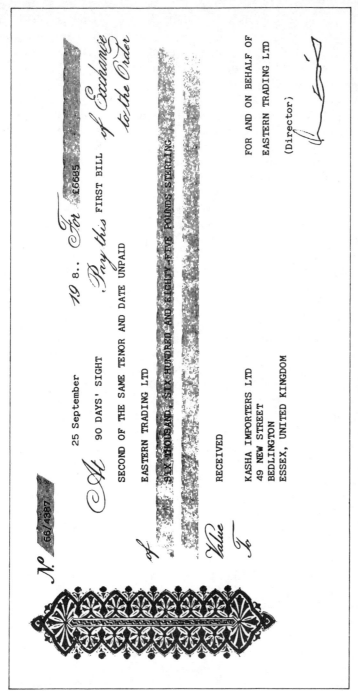

Figure 4.2 *Term draft – payable at 90 days after sight*

There are two kinds of draft: first, *sight drafts* which are payable at sight, or in practice within two banking days, and second, *term drafts* which are payable at so many days after sight, calculated in multiples of 30 days (ie 30, 60, 90 and so on up to, normally, 180 days).

If you receive a sight draft you pay at once and you get the documents and then can claim the goods. If you receive a term draft you write 'Accepted' on it and sign it, whereupon you receive the documents but pay on the due date in the future. At this point the draft becomes a bill of exchange. The UK bank will remit the proceeds to the supplier in his own country, and the transaction is complete.

You will appreciate that this is a far better deal for you, because you are not paying until you receive the goods, or at some time after you get them — that is, you are getting credit from your supplier. On the other hand it is not such a good deal for him because he does not get paid until the goods reach you, or some time afterwards, while he is unsure if you will pay the draft at all. He can instruct his bank that in the case of a shipment by sea the bill of lading is to be withheld, so you cannot get the goods. With a term draft you are given the bill of lading on agreeing to pay. Should you refuse to pay a draft when it is due, you would destroy your credit rating and your supplier would be able to take you to court for non-payment.

Suppliers overseas will normally deal with customers in the UK on these terms if they know them, and wish to extend credit to them. You can ask to pay this way, and if you have bought in the past from the supplier and paid promptly he may well agree. He may also allow credit, although he can include the cost of such credit in his quoted price. Or he may ask for interest on the amount of the accepted draft, which he would indicate on the draft itself.

If drafts are drawn in an importer's currency they will normally be payable at the current rate of exchange for drafts payable in the UK, a rate quoted daily by the banks.

The International Chamber of Commerce has issued a standard code of practice for drafts or bills of exchange, 'The Uniform Rules for the Collection of Paper', document 322, under which any disputes may be settled.

4. Open account

When you have become an established importer and are well known to your supplier overseas you may feel that you should be treated on the same basis as a domestic purchaser. This means you pay some time after receiving an invoice, such as the end of the month following receipt of the invoice. Buying from overseas, you will pay some time after receiving the documents and goods. Note that payment by purchasers within Europe is not normally made on the receipt of invoices, but usually involves some document equivalent to our bill of exchange, so that a definite date for payment is agreed, and you should not object to this if you are going to pay on the due date. It is only the purchasers who intend taking additional credit who dislike having a draft drawn on them.

If no draft is drawn on you, payment would be made by your bank on your instructions by having the money credited to your supplier's bank, probably by SWIFT or telegraphic transfer.

This method of payment is the best for you, because you have time in which to pay, but it is not so good for your supplier who is providing reasonably long credit, and he may well include the cost of this in his quoted price to you. It is much used by European suppliers to customers also in Europe, and between regular customers and suppliers who know and trust each other, since it saves many documentation costs.

5. Consignment stock

It is possible that you may wish to become the agent or distributor for your supplier, and act for him in the UK. If you are in the fast-moving consumer goods business (FMCG) you may find that to import such goods and resell them to retailers in the UK is difficult, because the retailers do not want any more such goods in their stores. If the imports cannot be stocked by retailers they may never be sold, so in these cases the only way out is to supply them to retailers on a sale or return basis (assuming they will agree to this).

If you buy such goods from a supplier overseas, you may feel reluctant to pay for them, since you have little idea if you can resell them, so you ask to have the goods 'on consignment' from the supplier overseas. This means the goods remain his property but are sent to you to distribute. You do not pay for them until they have been sold, and you have been paid by the retailers. A price is agreed with your supplier which includes an agreed margin of profit for you, and it is at this price that you then account to your supplier for the goods sold, say at the end of each month. He has no assurance that the goods

SPECIMEN INVOICE (clients' names are fictitious)

EASTERN TRADING Ltd

P O Box 500, MARINE PARADE POST OFFICE, SINGAPORE 9144
REPUBLIC OF SINGAPORE

Kasha Importers Ltd
49 New Street
Bedlington
Essex
United Kingdom

Date   18 August 198..

INVOICE No.   634781

QUANTITY	DESCRIPTION	AMOUNT	
560	Leather belts	1380	00
500	Leather straps	855	00
440	Leather handbags	3520	00
		£5755	00
	FREIGHT AT COST		
	36 cardboard cartons KIL Dover 1–36		

For and on behalf of
EASTERN TRADING LTD

Place and date of issue
SINGAPORE, 18.6.198..

Signature

(Commercial Manager)

Figure 4.3 *Invoice*

will be sold, but you do not pay him until they are. Not a very satisfactory way of doing business except in unusual circumstances, so neither exporters nor importers are keen to use it. We do not recommend it, but it may occur and is a method of payment you may have to use. You would arrange to pay as for open account.

6. Cash on delivery
Goods sent through the post may be sent on these terms, which means the post office collects the money for them before handing the goods over to you. Some airlines also offer a similar service, although this is not often used by exporters. We suggest it is better if you negotiate with your suppliers to pay by one of the other methods we have outlined, rather than cash on delivery.

7. Countertrade
As a small business you are unlikely ever to engage in countertrade, that is, exchanging goods instead of buying and paying for them (so that no money changes hands) but it is possible that an offer to supply goods as payment for your own purchases will arise, so you should be aware of the possibility. For example, if a supplier in an overseas country, short of foreign exchange, were desperate to buy certain goods from the UK but could not get the sterling to pay for them, you might offer to supply them, and thus pay for the goods you are buying in from that country. You would have to buy the goods he wants from a UK supplier, add on a margin of profit for yourself, then offer them to your supplier at that price, and have it set against what you owe him for your purchases.

Textiles have been bought from Romania, and paid for by selling the supplier bottles of tomato sauce. A price for the textiles was agreed in terms of tomato sauce. After the deal went through the supplier was able to sell the tomato sauce in Romania at a vast profit, where it was considered a luxury and certainly not normally imported from the UK.

Moreover, offering to sell at the same time as you offer to buy may help you to negotiate better terms for your purchases, especially as it may enable your supplier to make more money on what he buys from you, when he comes to resell those goods locally. Because of problems with obtaining foreign exchange many countries are encouraging various forms of countertrade. Indonesia, for instance, at present insists that import deals are matched by equivalent export deals.

Such deals can become complicated when the supplier does not want the goods offered by the customer, but can sell them to a third party for disposal elsewhere. This kind of deal usually involves an outside factor, but leaving this aside we always feel that any opportunity of helping others make money will in the end be to your advantage.

Foreign exchange

As a UK customer you can only pay a supplier overseas in sterling, because that is the currency we all use in Britain. The only currency your supplier can use is his own, eg American dollars for a supplier in the USA, or Swiss francs for a supplier in Switzerland.

Customers paying in their own currency will therefore have to change this into the supplier's currency. This is done on the foreign exchange market. Two factors are important here, one being whether your sterling can be changed into your supplier's francs or dollars etc, and the other being at what rate the exchange will be made. You can see at once that you might not be able to pay for your purchases if your sterling could not be changed into, say, rupees for Sri Lanka. And second, if you are quoted a price from a supplier overseas in his currency and you mentally convert this to sterling (to evaluate the cost of the goods to you), when you come to pay for the goods you might find the rate of exchange has moved against you, as we explained when dealing with quotations and orders in Chapter 2.

The first problem, namely that your supplier cannot be paid in his currency because you cannot buy it with your sterling, is both fairly remote (since sterling is at present freely convertible overseas), and a risk which your supplier takes, since he is the one who suffers if you cannot pay him for this reason. Provided you pay cash in advance, or by a confirmed documentary letter of credit, he runs no risk of not being paid, since the payment is already with him, in his own currency, in his country before he despatches the goods. This is why we suggested you should always offer to pay by means of a confirmed letter of credit, because an unconfirmed one does carry the risk that it might not be paid if the sterling could not then be converted or transferred to the supplier's bank in his currency.

With drafts, open account, or consignment stock the supplier takes the risk of not being paid because the sterling cannot be converted or transferred, and he will have to take out some form of credit insurance to see that he does. In Britain this risk is taken by the government's Export Credits Guarantee Department which protects a British exporter against non-payment by an overseas importer, and most countries have a similar kind of organisation. If your supplier fears that this situation may arise he may insist on payment by confirmed letter of credit or cash in advance; you must respect his fears should he be unable to insure against them, when you pay by means of a draft drawn on you, or by open account.

From your point of view the more serious risk is the rate of exchange going against you when you come to pay, and this may happen when you pay by any means other than cash in advance. The problem is to decide in which currency payment and, of course, orders and quotations, are agreed. You will prefer orders and payment to be in sterling, because you then know exactly what you are paying for the goods. But your customer may quote in his currency and, moreover, expect payment in it. This means he wants a letter of credit made out in his currency, or he may demand payment by means of a draft payable in his currency, and in both these cases you take the exchange risk. Of course, you also take the chance that the exchange may go in your favour, in which case you would be paying less for your goods than you actually agreed. But our advice to you is not to gamble; 'playing the currency market' can be a very dangerous game.

So if you accept quotations and place orders in your supplier's currency and also agree to pay in that currency, you must lay off the risk of a loss on the foreign exchange. You can do this by making a contract with your bank, which you must honour. It will ensure that you do not lose, whatever happens to the rate of exchange between sterling and your supplier's currency.

This contract is called a *forward exchange contract*, and is binding on both sides. You on your part guarantee to sell the sum you owe for the goods in sterling to the bank on a certain date, or between certain dates in the future, and to buy the equivalent amount of your supplier's currency with which to pay him. The bank on their part agree the rate of exchange at which the deal will be completed, and they will deal at this rate whatever the rate of exchange happens to be on the date or between the dates agreed. You can, as we say, deal on a definite nominated date, or on what is called an option, that is, between certain agreed dates, say between 1 and 30 November, which gives you the right to conclude the contract on any date you choose between those two dates.

As to the rate of exchange there are, as you may know, several: one for selling and one for buying; another for spot dealings (that is, immediate deals) or for forward deals (that is, at some date up to six months in the future). The bank, when you make this forward contract with them, will quote you the forward rate for selling sterling and buying your supplier's currency. So you know exactly at what rate you will have to pay, and it is at this forward rate that you agree the amount you will pay in your supplier's currency when you finally send him the order. Ensure that you make a definite payment date or an option between dates when you are sure you will be paying, because you cannot refuse to complete the contract.

The great advantage to you is that you know you cannot lose on the exchange, so you can happily agree to pay in your supplier's currency without risk. Therefore, you can open your letter of credit in your supplier's currency at this forward rate; you can accept a draft drawn on you by your supplier in his currency; and you can agree to pay in his currency on open account terms, nominating the dates between which you will pay.

Consult your bank about forward exchange contracts, which are available in all major currencies for periods up to about six months. And then apply the forward rates to your orders and the agreed method of payment. You can then see that when and how you pay affects the price you pay and the currency in which you pay.

Cost of money

You should already be familiar with the cost of money in your domestic business, but when it comes to importing it assumes even greater importance because of the time it will take for you to place an order, and then finally receive and pay for the goods. When you pay, compared with when you actually receive the goods, means that you must calculate the cost of tying up your money for some period of time, and this is done as follows:

Assume the cost of money (ie the cost of borrowing it) to be 20 per cent pa. If you buy £1000-worth of goods and you have to pay for them, say, 90 days before you actually receive them (eg because you have opened a letter of credit that far in advance), then the fomula you use is:

$$\frac{90 \times 20}{365} = 5\%.$$

That is, you multiply the number of days' credit by the cost of the money and divide by the number of days in a year. Then turn this percentage into a fraction, 1/20. Deduct one figure from the lower number, 1/19, and if you apply this to the £1000, you get £52.63. That is the cost to you of being out of your £1000 for 90 days, at today's cost of money.

Your supplier, if he gives you 90 days' credit, may well have included this in his price to you. If you have to pay 90 days in advance then this is the additional cost of the goods to you. If you pay for goods when you receive them, and do not get your money back by reselling them for 90 days, then this is also the additional cost to you. You will have many of these calculations to make before finally arriving at the cost of the goods you buy from overseas, because you must take into account what money costs when you use it to buy abroad.

You can now see how important a factor in any imports is the method of payment, because in the first place it affects the cost of the goods to you, and hence the price you agree to pay for them. This is, of course, not quite the end so far as costs and prices are concerned because there are additional ones in the form of unloading, clearing and documentation charges, plus customs duty, VAT, and inland transport charges. These will all be dealt with in succeeding chapters, and the final costs and prices in Chapter 9.

Second, you must appreciate how important your own creditworthiness is if you wish to obtain the best possible terms from your suppliers overseas. These will certainly reflect the confidence they have in your ability and willingness to pay as and when agreed in the contract to buy.

Third, you can see that whichever method of payment your supplier will accept must affect your cash flow, so the longer you have to pay, the better.

Fourth, *when* you pay affects your costs, and this should be a bargaining point with your suppliers. They should know the rules, but you must take the initiative as the buyer, and suggest the method of payment which suits you best.

Fifth, you must decide the currency of the contract and

the currency in which it is to be calculated, ensuring that you do not lose because of any changes in the rate of exchange by making forward contracts with your bank if necessary.

Lastly, before concluding any deal to buy from a supplier overseas, make sure you have negotiated as well as you can on how and when you will pay, because of the importance to you of these two points. We will have more to say about the art of negotiating deals with suppliers overseas in the last chapter of this book.

Chapter 5

Import Regulations and Controls

In Chapter 1 we touched briefly on UK import controls, while we also raised the question of the special requirements of HM Customs and Excise, the Department of Trade and Industry etc. This, as you will appreciate, is a detailed and complicated subject, and to keep up to date you will need to make regular checks with the authorities concerned. While this may sound like a good deal of hard work, in practice you need only concern yourself with a small part of the regulations as they apply to your particular business. However, to give you some idea of how imports are regulated and controlled, here is a summary of the position at the time of writing.

Import regulations

Imports are regulated by the government for economic, social, financial or political reasons. If the government wants to encourage free trade, there will be few controls over what you import and from which countries; but if the government wants to protect home industries, then it will impose strict limits on imported goods.

No government, however, can act entirely as it likes because Britain has made certain agreements with other countries, and these would have to be broken before any unilateral action could be taken to impose stricter import regulations and controls. The first is the international multilateral agreement known as GATT (General Agreement on Tariffs and Trade). The signatories, which include most countries in the world, have agreed to liberalise their trade by reducing tariffs and other barriers to trade, such as import quotas, restrictions on the use of foreign currency and various regulations affecting imported goods (eg having special exhaust systems fitted to imported cars for the USA). Moreover, the United Nations have also set up UNCTAD (United Nations Conference on Trade and Development) with the object of helping developing nations to gain easier access to the more developed markets of the world.

In addition to the United Nations' regulations, as a member of the EC (European Community) Britain is bound by the Community's regulations on imports both from other members and from those countries associated with the Community. There are, as you will know, 12 members of the Community, namely France, the Federal Republic of Germany, Italy, Belgium, Holland, Luxembourg, Denmark, Greece, the Republic of Ireland, Spain and Portugal, and the United Kingdom.

As a member of the EC Britain is obliged to allow most goods from other member states into the country free of customs duty because they are deemed to be of 'Community origin'. The definition of Community origin is that the goods are 'wholly obtained' in the Community, or they are produced there wholly or partly from imported materials and parts, provided that all duties have been paid on these goods when they entered the Community and no duty is reclaimed (drawback) when they leave the UK. The goods are then in 'free circulation', that is, they can move freely between member states without payment of customs duties. This is because all member states of the Community charge the same rate of duty on imported goods (the CCT – Common Customs Tariff). Therefore, goods bear the same rate of duty no matter into which EC country they are imported. However, excise duty is still payable; this is charged on imported and home-produced goods at the same rate (eg wines and spirits would come in duty free from France, but the excise duty would be levied on French brandy at the same rate as it is on Scotch whisky). Also, VAT is payable as it is on UK goods.

As an example, furniture made in Denmark from Danish wood can be imported into Britain duty free, as also can furniture made in France from Danish wood. So could furniture made in Denmark from wood imported from outside the Community provided it had paid the common customs duty, and no drawback on that duty had been claimed.

This rule of origin, with minor variations, is true in all trading agreements we have, as set out in Public Notice 826, 'European Community Preferences – Imports', and 828 'EEC Preferences: Rules of Origin'. While these Community rules apply to most products, there are certain sensitive ones, such as paper and board products, which still attract import duties, while other goods may be subject to quotas and ceilings, and duties can always be re-imposed at any time by the Community.

These Community regulations also apply to industrial goods imported by any Community member state from any of the seven European Free Trade Area (EFTA) countries, namely Austria, Finland, Iceland, Norway, Sweden and Switzerland (including Liechtenstein). It is in fact to these countries that Notice 828 above applies. Goods may be imported from these EFTA countries if they were wholly produced there, or from materials produced there; but if the materials came from outside, then they would have to comply with certain rules, which are extremely complicated, but with which your exporter has to deal and supply documentary evidence. For example, you can import furniture from Norway made of Norwegian wood duty free, but not if the wood had been grown in Taiwan and made up in Norway.

In addition to these seven EFTA countries, the Community has similar arrangements with a number of associated countries, whereby goods can enter the Community either free of duty or at reduced rates. The two groups of countries are first, the 'Maghreb' countries of Algeria, Morocco and Tunisia, and second, the 'Mashraq' countries of Egypt, Jordan, Lebanon, Syria and the Faroe Islands.

The Community has extended its preferential regulations to a great many other countries in an endeavour to help them to trade with the affluent countries of western Europe, and thus goods imported from these countries pay either no duty or a reduced rate. There are a great many of these developing countries, of whom you will probably have heard of the ACP group (ie African, Caribbean and Pacific countries) which have been most active in soliciting help from the Community, beginning with the great Lomé conference. Then there are a number of OCTs (Overseas Countries and Territories) which include such countries as St Helena, the Cayman Islands, Belize, Pitcairn, St Pierre and Miquelon. There are also the GSP (Generalised System of Preferences) countries with whom we have signed trading agreements to encourage their exports. So if you import from practically any of the developing nations in the groups ACP, OCT or GSP, there will be little or no duty payable. For specific details, apply to your local office of HM Customs and Excise.

The exporter has the responsibility of sending you documentary evidence to enable you to import goods free of duty, and he may send you the relevant sheets of the Single Administrative Document (SAD) if the goods come from a full

69

Community member state, an EUR 1 or an invoice declaration form if they come from EFTA or A forms if from other countries (see Chapter 6).

Your main responsibility is to check:

1. Can your goods enter free of duty?
2. Can they enter at a reduced duty?
3. Are the goods subject to any Community ceilings (ie are they within import levels of previous years)?
4. Are they within the limit of the UK share of the Community tariff quota?
5. Are they subject to any limitation known as the 'butoir', which states that goods of one developing nation may not take up more than a certain percentage of the overall Community tariff quota for a particular product?

One important point concerning the evidence required when the goods enter Britain, should this not be available from your supplier: you can still claim reduced duties or duty free, and customs will provisionally release the goods subject to your giving them a security or deposit equal to the full amount of customs duties payable if preference is not allowed. Alternatively, you can give them a guarantee, backed by your bank, that you undertake to produce the necessary documents in support of your claim for a preferential rate of duty, or pay that duty within four months of the entry being lodged. You specify the goods, how they were imported, their value, and you add your own name as importer (or that of your import agent) and to this declaration the bank adds its own guarantee; the bank must of course be one approved by the customs.

We said that these customs regulations sound more complicated than they are, but as a small importer you will only be concerned with a few goods from a limited number of countries. So all you need to get from customs is the regulation covering those specific countries and goods and abide by that.

Import controls

In addition to the problems of import regulations, you must become familiar with the various import controls, some of which we have briefly mentioned in Chapter 1.

As we said, an import licence is needed before any goods may be imported into Britain with the following exceptions:

1. Trade samples.
2. Goods returned to the country, eg after use by the owner if he has hired them and is now returning them to the supplier in the UK.
3. Goods imported into the UK for repair and subsequent re-export.
4. Personal and household effects.
5. Printed trade advertising material.
6. Privately owned motor vehicles.
7. Gifts (provided they are genuine gifts).

Imports from the Channel Islands are exempted from licensing rules, except for arms, ammunition, dyes, dyestuffs and plumage.

The import licence is obtained from the Import Licensing Branch of the Department of Trade and Industry, and in many cases is a mere formality. Most goods can be imported under an Open General Licence, which means you do not have to apply for an import licence, and you should check with the Department to see whether your imports come under this general category. There may be exceptions, listed in Schedules 1, 2 and 3 to the Open General Licence, which prohibit the import of particular goods at certain times, eg new potatoes cannot be imported between 1 November and 31 August. In addition, dangerous drugs and live animals are subject to restrictions or prohibition. You can find details of these various import controls in *Croner's Reference Book for Importers*.

Should your goods require an import licence, then this may be one of three kinds. An *Open Individual Import Licence* allows you to bring in specified goods without limit on quantity or value from the stated source, for the period of the licence, or until it is revoked. Second, there is a *Specific Import Licence*, which will be for a stated period and a specified value, allowing you to import a particular product from a stated source. Third, a *Surveillance Licence* will be needed for all goods subject to the Community surveillance licensing restrictions, which come into the UK from outside the Community.

Each import licence will have an expiry date, by which time the goods must have been imported. Extensions are not automatically granted, and any application for an extension must be made to the Import Licensing Branch of the Department of Trade and Industry before the goods leave the exporting country, while full reasons for the cause of the delay must be given.

When you import goods these must be marked in the same

way as the equivalent goods produced in this country, this being a requirement of the Trade Descriptions Acts of 1968 and 1972. For example, if the imported goods have a name which would be liable to be confused with that of a British manufacturer, then the country of origin of the imported goods must be clearly shown in conspicuous lettering. *Croner's* shows you the details.

There are five categories of goods requiring the country of origin to be clearly shown, namely textiles, clothing, footwear, cutlery and electrical appliances. Where goods are advertised to retail customers their country of origin must also be clearly stated.

You should remember that HM Customs and Excise do not fix the rates of duty, they merely collect them. Therefore they need accurate, written information about the goods, and they have the right to inspect them at any time. They also check that a relevant import licence has been granted if required, and they will check to see that no limitations or restrictions have been broken. They are concerned to prevent the smuggling of prohibited goods (such as drugs) into the country, and they are also responsible for collecting and processing information about all goods imported, from which the national trade figures are compiled. They also do this for exports, so they provide the information for both exports and imports, and thus assess the balance of trade of the UK.

Customs clearance

As an importer you are responsible for clearing your imported goods through customs, provided that the terms of delivery under which you bought the goods overseas are such that the supplier does not have to do this for you (see Chapter 2). Depending on which terms of delivery you have bought, your task will be to:

1. Pay any port charges.
2. Prepare customs documents, and pay the customs duty.
3. Pay any local transport charges.
4. Arrange for the goods to be delivered to you from the port or airport.
5. Arrange for the goods to be insured.

As we have already said in Chapter 3, you will probably need the services of a freight forwarder to act as your import agent, and he will arrange to clear the goods through customs, as well as attend to the other tasks set out above.

Before we can proceed any further, however, there are other shipping documents which will be required by you from your suppliers, and these we shall consider briefly in Chapter 6. We must then consider the duties and reliefs payable on imported goods in Chapter 7, and finally have a look at clearing goods through customs in some detail, which we will do in Chapter 8.

Shipping Documents

When you import goods directly from overseas your supplier —
that is the exporter of the goods you are buying — will usually
be responsible for sending you the goods and their documents,
depending on the terms of delivery under which you bought
them. In certain cases, however, *you* may arrange for the
despatch of the goods, in which case you would be responsible
for preparing what are loosely called the 'shipping documents',
or your freight forwarder would if he were handling the transport of the goods for you. These documents enable you to have
the goods transported, insured, and delivered to your own
premises, and are also needed to have the goods cleared through
customs and pass any other import formalities.

How you are paying for the goods may affect how these
documents are sent to you since, if you are paying by documentary letter of credit, you have to specify both the documents
you need and how they are to be sent to you. But if your
supplier is drawing a draft on you, which you have either to pay
or accept, then he will arrange for the documents to be handed
over to you, in exchange for your payment or agreement to
pay the draft (see Chapter 4). So the two problems for the
importer are first, what documents are needed, and second, how
you can obtain these documents.

In previous chapters we have referred to most of these documents, but because they are so important to you it seems
sensible to go over them again, and to remind you that it is
your responsibility to instruct your suppliers as to precisely
which documents you require. If the documents are incorrect
or incomplete you will have difficulty in getting your goods,
and you might have to provide an indemnity (ie, a financial
guarantee) to the authorities before they will release the consignment to you. Or you may only get them by paying a deposit.
So from the outset, when you order goods from overseas, make
sure you specify in detail exactly what documents you will
need, and how many of each must be prepared. Exporters are

taught documentation, but from experience we all know how many exporters ignore instructions and submit either wrong or inaccurate documents. For example, over 60 per cent of the documents presented to the banks in this country by British exporters trading on documentary letters of credit are rejected because they are wrong. And exporters in other countries are not likely to be more efficient. You may even consider that the service you get from a supplier in the matter of documents will, to some degree, determine whether that supplier gets the order or not, because inefficient service should not be tolerated by a buyer.

Shipping documents in common use

The documents which are commonly used for the shipment of goods from one country to another are as follows:

Invoices. An invoice in international trade is not a demand for payment but a record of goods sent, and evidence of a contract. When you import you will need invoices from your buyer showing details of the goods supplied and their price. If the supplier has despatched the goods he must also show details of the freight and insurance as separate items. These invoices must be certified as correct as regards the value and origin of the goods, and you will need additional copies for HM Customs, so you must insist on having the right number of invoices sent to you.

Certificates of origin. Normally these are not specifically required, but where preferential rates of duty are being claimed you will need a certificate of origin, issued and signed by a Chamber of Commerce in the supplier's country. You will find details of which countries this applies to in *Croner's Reference Book for Importers.* Your suppliers should know this, but it is better if you tell them as well.

Packing list. Where different goods are ordered in one consignment, but are packed in several cases, you and the customs may wish to identify which goods are in each case. You may also wish to check their condition for insurance purposes. In these instances a packing list is essential, so unless you are ordering a single item we suggest you include a packing list in the list of documents you require.

Transport documents. We referred in Chapter 3 to transport

1 Absender · Consignor · Expediteur · Expedidor	**B** 0478236		**ORIGINAL**
	EUROPÄISCHE GEMEINSCHAFT EUROPEAN COMMUNITY · COMMUNAUTE EUROPEENNE COMUNIDAD EUROPEA		
2 Empfänger · Consignee · Destinataire · Destinatario	**URSPRUNGSZEUGNIS** CERTIFICATE OF ORIGIN · CERTIFICAT D'ORIGINE CERTIFICADO DE ORIGEN		
	3 Ursprungsland · Country of origin · Pays d'origine · Pais de origen		
4 Angaben über die Beförderung · means of transport · expédition · expedición	5 Bemerkungen · remarks · observations · observaciones		

6 Laufende Nummer; Zeichen, Nummern, Anzahl und Art der Packstucke · Warenbezeichnung	7 Menge

8 DIE UNTERZEICHNENDE STELLE BESCHEINIGT, DASS DIE OBEN BEZEICHNETEN WAREN IHREN URSPRUNG IN DEM IN FELD 3 GENANNTEN LAND HABEN

The undersigned authority certifies that the goods described above originate in the country shown in box 3
L'autorité soussignée certifie que les marchandises désignées ci-dessus sont originaires du pays figurant dans la case No 3
La autoridad infrascrita certifica que las mercancias abajo mencionadas son originarias del pais que figura en la casilla no 3

Ort und Datum der Ausstellung · Bezeichnung · Unterschrift und Stempel der zuständigen Stelle

Verlag Hanswalter Bensemann 1126 D-6253 Hadamar ☎ (06433) 23 45
EWG-Ursprungszeugnis Bestell-Nr. 3200

Druck genehmigt durch Erlaß des Bundesministers der Finanzen vom 22 5 1969 III B / 8   2 · 151   27 · 69

Figure 6.1 *EC Certificate of Origin*

76

ORIGINAL

1. Goods consigned from (Exporter's business name, address, country) MEHRA H.K. Ching San Lane 848 Chung Hom Kok Road, Hong Kong	Reference No. 85/67821 GENERALISED SYSTEM OF PREFERENCES **CERTIFICATE OF ORIGIN** (Combined declaration and certificate) **FORM A**
2. Goods consigned to (Consignee's name, address, country) Kasha Importers Ltd 49 New Street Bedlington Essex , United Kingdom	Issued in Hong Kong (country) See Notes overleaf
3. Means of transport and route (as far as known) First available transport	4. For official use

5. Item number	6. Marks and numbers of packages	7. Number and kind of packages; description of goods	8. Origin criterion (see Notes overleaf)	9. Gross weight or other quantity	10. Number and date of invoices
1	KIL Felixstowe 1-100	100 cartons Children's clothing	'P'	1100 articles	3451 18.6.198..

SPECIMEN

11. **Certification** It is hereby certified, on the basis of control carried out, that the declaration by the exporter is correct.	12. **Declaration by the exporter** The undersigned hereby declares that the above details and statements are correct; that all the goods were produced in Hong Kong (country) and that they comply with the origin requirements specified for those goods in the Generalised System of Preferences for goods exported to United Kingdom (importing country) Hong Kong, 18.6.198..
Place and date, signature and stamp of certifying authority	Place and date, signature of authorised signatory

Figure 6.2 *Form A, as sent to the importer
in order to claim entry duty free or at a reduced rate of duty*

This page to be completed by the Exporter   G.S.P.

EXPORTER (Full Name & Address)	香 港 總 商 會
Mehra H.K Ching San Lane, 848 Chung Hom Kok Road, Hong Kong B.R. No. 83521/36 Tel. No. 5-0118529	THE HONG KONG GENERAL CHAMBER OF COMMERCE 本商會認由香港政府根據1967年非政府產地來源證保護法例授權簽發產地來源證。 Authorised by the Government of Hong Kong to issue Certificates of Origin under the Protection of Non- Government Certificates of Origin Ordinance, 1967.

Application to The Hong Kong General Chamber of Commerce by an Exporter for a Certificate of Origin Form A and declarations by a *Manufacturer/Producer/Subcontractor and Exporter in support thereof

1. I ...V. J. Mehra................................... * Proprietor
            (Insert Name)   Partner   of the above-named exporting firm, the exporter of the
                          Principal Official

merchandise specified in this application, apply for a **CERTIFICATE OF ORIGIN FORM A** and hereby declare:—

  (a) that I am duly authorized to make and sign this declaration on behalf of the above-named exporting firm;
  (b) that the merchandise described below consists exclusively of the goods *manufactured/produced by the *manufacturer/producer/subcontractor described overleaf and will be exported by me in the manner described below;
  (c) that I *have/have not applied to any other Issuing Authority for a Certificate of Origin in respect of the consignment described hereunder;
  (d) that all the information I have given in this application is true and correct.   * Delete wherever inapplicable.

Carrier Orient/Occident Line	Sea/Airport of Loading Hong Kong	Departure/Closing Date 20.7.198..	Country of Destination & Code No. England
Port of Discharge Felixstowe	Final Destination if on Carriage Bedlington		If the goods do not carry any labels or brand names the word "none" should be inserted.

Mark(s) & Number(s)	No. of Packages & Description of Goods	Quantity or Weight & Unit Price (FOB Value)	Total FOB value (HK$)	Brand names or labels
CTR No. BML 3063231 SEAL NO. 34462 KIL Felixstowe 1 - 100	100 cartons Children's clothing	1100 articles	43,550	None

2. Should samples of the goods under application be required for scrutiny, these may be obtained by contacting

Mr. ...V. J. Mehra............................... Tel. No. 5-0118529.....
*(Signatures and English translations of Chinese character
signatures should be repeated in block capitals.)*

                           Authorized Signature:— ....
                           & Company Chop
                           Date ....18.6................19.....

Note 1. This application and declaration must be made personally by the proprietor or by a partner or principal official authorized by the firm or company exporting the goods.

Note 2. It must be presented to THE HONG KONG GENERAL CHAMBER OF COMMERCE at least 2 clear working days in advance of the advertised departure date of the vessel concerned.

Note 3. The penalty for making a false declaration in respect of a Certificate of Origin Form A is $50,000 and one year's imprisonment. The penalty for substitution of goods in respect of a Certificate of Origin Form A is $100,000 and one year's imprisonment.

Accepted	Remarks	Date and Number

Figure 6.3 *Declaration of Origin — attached to Form A — provided by the exporter to comply with origin requirements*

Declaration by *Manufacturer/Producer

1. I .... of ....
   (Insert Name)   *(Insert Name of Factory)*

   hereby declare that the goods which are fully and accurately described below have been *manufactured/produced in the premises or place in Hong Kong registered with the Trade Department as factory No. .... situated at
   ....

Marks, Nos. and Container No.; No. and Kind of Packages; Description of Goods	No. of Units & Unit Price	Total Selling Price to Exporter	Brand Names or Labels

2. Full description and origin of the materials and/or component parts used in the *manufacture/production of the articles described above are as follows:—

Materials/Component Parts	Country of Origin	Materials/Component Parts	Country of Origin

3. The work done IN HONG KONG to transform the materials and/or component parts detailed in para. 2 above into the goods described in para. I above is as follows:—

(A) In the above-mentioned factory:— ....
   ....

(B) By subcontractor in Hong Kong (See Note 1):—

  (i) Entire production/terminal processes of manufacture approved by Director of Trade as follows:

    (a) Trade Department Approval Reference No.: ....

    (b) Name, Address and Trade Department factory registration number of subcontractor: ....
   ....
   ....

    (c) Processes carried out by the above-mentioned subcontractor:
   ....
   ....
   ....

    (d) Quantity: ....

  (ii) Intermediate processes of manufacture to factories approved by Director of Trade under Reference No..

  (iii) Intermediate processes of manufacture to the following factories for which prior approval from the Director of Trade has not been obtained (Names and addresses to be given):—

(C) By outworkers (See Note 1):— ....

4. The work done OUTSIDE HONG KONG in connection with the manufacture of the goods described in para. 1 above is as follows (if applicable):

    Processes Carried Out   *Country of Operation*
   ....
   ....
   ....

> **Declaration by Subcontractor**
>
> I,...
> principal official of ....
> ....
> *(Insert Name of Subcontractor's Factory)*
> hereby declare that I have carried out the manufacturing process(es) in my factory as described in para. 3 (B) (i) of the declaration by the manufacturer/producer on this page.
>
> Date ....
>   *Signature & Factory Chop*

5. The goods have been wholly produced or have undergone working, processing or assembly in Hong Kong as a result of which the following requirements have been met:

6. The goods are for export by.. of ....
          (name of exporting firm)   *(address of exporting firm)*

* and have been processed to the order of..
* Delete wherever inapplicable.   *(Insert Name of firm)*

7. For at least 2 clear working days following the date of this application the goods will be at..
   ....where they will be available for inspection.
   (address where goods may be inspected before shipment)

8. I hereby declare that all the particulars set out in paragraphs 1-7 above were supplied by me and that they are true and correct.
   本人茲宣誓證明本申請書第（一）段至第（七）段開列之全部資料，均由本人提供，而該等資料全屬正確無訛。

Authorized Signature:—   Office Address: ....
& Factory Chop   ....
(Signatures and English translations of Chinese character signatures should be repeated in block capitals.)   ....

Date 19   Tel. No. ....

Note 1. In case where any process involving the manufacture and production of goods is performed in premises other than those stated at para. 1 above, the declarant must provide full particulars regarding the process at paragraphs 3 (B), 3 (C) and/or 4 as appropriate.

Note 2. The penalty for making a false declaration in respect of a Certificate of Origin Form A is $50,000 and one year's imprisonment. The penalty for substitution of goods in respect of a Certificate of Origin Form A is $100,000 and one year's imprisonment.

Figure 6.3 *Declaration of Origin (reverse)*

documents, and you will remember that in the case of shipments by sea you must be in possession of a bill of lading made out to you, or 'to order', and endorsed to you, if you wish to obtain a delivery order for the goods from the shipping line. If you are paying by letter of credit you normally specify a full set of 'clean, on board bills of lading', showing that the goods were shipped on the named ship, and that they were in apparent good order and condition when loaded.

In the case of shipments by air, road or rail you will not need the air waybill, CMR or CIM to obtain delivery, because the goods will be delivered to you. You will need the air waybill number if you collect them from the airport. You will receive these documents in due course, however, because they are your receipts for the goods and your contracts of carriage with the carriers. A parcel post receipt will be sent to you, but the post office will deliver if the goods are less than £50 in value.

Import licence. As we saw in Chapter 4 you may need one, and if so it must be attached to the rest of the shipping documents when the goods are being cleared on arrival.

Movement certificates. These, as we saw in the previous chapter, are important if the goods come into Britain at preferential rates of duty, so your supplier should send you one of the following:

☐ Certificate of Origin for Goods entitled to the Generalised System of Preferences (GSP) — Form A
☐ EUR 1 or EUR 2 for Preferential Trade Agreements (PTA) goods and for Spanish territories of Canary Islands, Ceuta and Melilla
☐ An invoice declaration or an EUR 1 for goods coming from EFTA.

These forms have to be completed and signed before the goods leave and, in many cases, have also to be signed by the local customs authorities.

Community transit documents. When you import from another EC country you will need a Single Administrative Document (SAD) to show that the goods are of Community origin and are in free circulation. The supplier will, via the haulier, send the relevant copies necessary for you to claim duty free entry into the UK.

WARENVERKEHRSBESCHEINIGUNG

1. Ausführer/Exporteur (Name, vollständige Anschrift, Staat)	**EUR. 1** Nr. **D** 217518
	Vor dem Ausfüllen Anmerkungen auf der Rückseite beachten
	2. Bescheinigung für den Präferenzverkehr zwischen
3. Empfänger (Name, vollständige Anschrift, Staat) (Ausfüllung freigestellt)	................Europäische Wirtschaftsgemeinschaft................ und dem in Feld 5 genannten Staat oder der dort genannten Staatengruppe (Angabe der betreffenden Staaten, Staatengruppen oder Gebiete)

4. Staat, Staatengruppe oder Gebiet, als dessen bzw. deren Ursprungswaren die Waren gelten	5. Bestimmungsstaat, -staatengruppe oder -gebiet
6. Angaben über die Beförderung (Ausfüllung freigestellt)	7. Bemerkungen

[1] Bei unverpackten Waren ist die Anzahl der Gegenstände oder „lose geschüttet" anzugeben.

8. Laufende Nr.; Zeichen, Nummern, Anzahl und Art der Packstücke [1]; Warenbezeichnung	9. Rohgewicht (kg) oder andere Maße (l. m³, usw.)	10. Rechnungen (Ausfüllung freigestellt)

[2] In der Bundesrepublik Deutschland vom Ausführer auszufüllen

11. SICHTVERMERK DER ZOLLBEHÖRDE	12. ERKLÄRUNG DES AUSFÜHRERS/ EXPORTEURS
Die Richtigkeit der Erklärung wird bescheinigt. Ausfuhrpapier:[2] Stempel Art/Muster .... Nr. .... vom................... Zollbehörde: .... Ausstellender/s Staat/Gebiet: .... **Bundesrepublik Deutschland** .... (Ort und Datum) .... (Unterschrift)	Der Unterzeichner erklärt, daß die vorgenannten Waren die Voraussetzungen erfüllen, um diese Bescheinigung zu erlangen. .... (Ort und Datum) .... (Unterschrift)

Figure 6.4 *EUR 1, used in trade between the EC and other preference-giving areas or countries*

81

FORMBLATT **EUR. 2** Nr. D 067356

1 Formblatt für den begünstigten Warenverkehr zwischen [1] der Europäischen Wirtschaftsgemeinschaft und dem in Feld 9 genannten Staat

2 Ausführer (Name, vollständige Anschrift, Staat)

3 Erklärung des Ausführers

Ich, der Unterzeichner, Ausführer der nachstehend bezeichneten Waren, erkläre, daß diese die für die Ausstellung dieses Formblatts geforderten Voraussetzungen erfüllen, und daß sie die Eigenschaft von Ursprungswaren gemäß den Bedingungen für den in Feld 1 genannten begünstigten Warenverkehr erworben haben.

4 Empfänger (Name, vollständige Anschrift, Staat)

5 Ort und Datum

6 Unterschrift des Ausführers

7 Bemerkungen [2]

8 Ursprungsstaat [3]

9 Bestimmungsstaat [4]

10 Rohgewicht (kg)

11 Zeichen, Nummern der Sendung und Warenbezeichnung

12 Behörde oder Dienststelle des Ausfuhrstaats [4], der die Nachprüfung der Erklärung des Ausführers obliegt

Der Bundesminister der Finanzen
– Referat III B 8 –
Graurheindorfer Straße 108
D - 5300 Bonn 1

Vor dem Ausfüllen des Formblatts sind die Hinweise auf der Rückseite sorgfältig zu lesen.

1) Angabe der betreffenden Staaten, Staatengruppen oder Gebiete. 2) Hinweise auf Prüfungen durch die zuständige Behörde oder Dienststelle, soweit sie schon stattgefunden haben. 3) Als Ursprungsstaat gilt der Staat, die Staatengruppe oder das Gebiet, als dessen bzw. deren Ursprungswaren die Waren gelten. 4) Als Staat gilt auch eine Staatengruppe oder ein Gebiet.

Figure 6.5 *EUR 2: can be used instead of EUR 1 for low value goods*

WARENVERKEHRSBESCHEINIGUNG

1. Ausführer (Name, vollständige Anschrift, Staat)	**A.TR. 1** Nr. **L** 609115
	Vor dem Ausfüllen Anmerkungen auf der Rückseite beachten
	2. Frachtbrief (Ausfüllung freigestellt) Nr. _____ vom _____
3. Empfänger (Name, vollständige Anschrift, Staat) (Ausfüllung freigestellt)	4. **ASSOZIATION** zwischen der **EUROPÄISCHEN WIRTSCHAFTSGEMEINSCHAFT** und der **TÜRKEI**
	5. Ausfuhrstaat	6. Bestimmungsstaat [1]
7. Angaben über die Beförderung (Ausfüllung freigestellt)	8. Bemerkungen [2]

Laufende Nr.	10. Zeichen, Nummern, Anzahl und Art der Packstücke (bei lose geschütteten Waren je nach Fall Name des Schiffes, Waggon- oder Kraftwagennummer); Warenbezeichnung	11. Rohgewicht (kg) oder andere Maße (hl, m³ usw.)

12. BESCHEINIGUNG DER ZOLLSTELLE	13. ERKLÄRUNG DES AUSFÜHRERS
Die Richtigkeit der Erklärung wird bescheinigt. Stempel Ausfuhrpapier: [3] Art/Muster _____ Nr. _____ vom _____ Zollstelle: _____ Ausstellender Staat: _____ (Ort und Datum) (Unterschrift)	Der Unterzeichner erklärt, daß die vorgenannten Waren die Voraussetzungen erfüllen, um diese Bescheinigung zu erlangen. (Ort und Datum) (Unterschrift)

Figure 6.6 *Form A.TR.1 used in trade with Turkey*

83

NOTE: Importers are advised to read this form and the notes thereto in Notice No 251 before making their declarations.
This form should not be signed before it is fully completed.

DECLARATION of Particulars relating to Customs Value   (Method 1)

1. Buyer (in BLOCK LETTERS)

FOR OFFICIAL USE (No. of entry)

2. Seller (in BLOCK LETTERS)

3. Number and date of invoice

4. Number and date of contract

5. Terms of delivery (e.g. fob New York)

6. Number and date of any previous Customs decision concerning boxes 7 to 9

Enter X where applicable

7.(a) Are the buyer and seller **related** in the sense of Article 1(2)* of Regulation (EEC) No. 1224/80? . . . . □ YES □ NO
If "NO", go to box 8

(b) Did the relationship **influence** the price of the imported goods? . . . . □ YES □ NO

(c) Does the transaction value of the imported goods **closely approximate** to a value mentioned
in Article 3(2)(b) of Regulation (EEC) No. 1224/80? . . . . □ YES □ NO
If "YES", give details:

8.(a) Are there any **restrictions** as to the disposition or use of the goods by the buyer, other than
restrictions which

—are imposed or required by law or by the public authorities in the Community,
—limit the geographical area in which the goods may be resold, or
—do not substantially affect the value of the goods? . . . . □ YES □ NO

(b) Is the sale or price subject to some **condition** or **consideration** for which a value cannot be determined
with respect to the goods being valued? . . . . □ YES □ NO
Specify the nature of the restrictions, conditions or considerations as appropriate.
If the value of such condition or consideration can be determined, indicate the amount in box 11(b) overleaf.

9.(a) Are any **royalties and licence fees** related to the imported goods payable either directly or indirectly by the
buyer as a condition of the sale? . . . . □ YES □ NO

(b) Is the sale subject to an arrangement under which part of the proceeds of any subsequent **resale**, disposal or
use accrues directly or indirectly to the seller? . . . . □ YES □ NO
If "YES" to either of these questions, specify conditions and, if possible, indicate the amounts in boxes 15 and 16
overleaf:

*Persons shall be deemed to be related only if:

(a) they are officers or directors of one another's businesses;

(b) they are legally recognised partners in business;

(c) they are employer and employee;

(d) any person directly or indirectly owns, controls or holds 5% or
more of the outstanding voting stock or shares or both of them;

(e) one of them directly or indirectly controls the other;

(f) both of them are directly or indirectly controlled by a third person;

(g) together they directly or indirectly control a third person;

(h) they are members of the same family.

10. I, the undersigned, declare that all particulars given in this
document are true and complete.

Place .... Date................ 19.....

Signature...

Declarant:

A

C 105A   F 990 (July, 1980)

Figure 6.7 *Form C105A, used for goods over a specified
value and subject to* ad valorem *duty*

		Item............	Item............	Item............
A. Basis of calculation	**11.** (a) † Net price in **currency of invoice** ... ... (b) Indirect payments — see box 8(b) overleaf (Rate of exchange.....................)..			
	12. TOTAL A in **National currency**			
B. Additions: Costs in **National currency NOT** included in A above*	**13.** Costs incurred by the buyer: (a) commissions, except buying commissions			
	(b) brokerage			
	(c) containers and packing			
Quote below previous relevant Customs decisions, if any: V /	**14.** Goods and services supplied by the buyer free of charge or at reduced cost for use in connection with the production and sale for export of the imported goods: The values shown represent an apportionment where appropriate. (a) materials, components, parts and similar items incorporated in the imported goods			
	(b) tools, dies, moulds and similar items used in the production of the imported goods			
	(c) materials consumed in the production of the imported goods ..			
	(d) engineering, development, artwork, design work, and plans and sketches undertaken elsewhere than in the Community and necessary for the production of the imported goods			
	15. Royalties and licence fees — see box 9(a) overleaf			
	16. Proceeds of any subsequent resale, disposal or use accruing to the seller — see box 9(b) overleaf			
	17. Costs of delivery to... (place of introduction) (a) transport			
	(b) loading and handling charges			
	(c) insurance			
	18. TOTAL B			
C. Deductions: Costs in **National currency** included in A above*	**19.** Costs of transport after importation			
	20. Charges for construction, erection, assembly, maintenance or technical assistance undertaken after importation			
	21. Other charges (specify)			
	22. Customs duties and taxes payable in the country of importation by reason of the importation or sale of the goods			
	23. TOTAL C			
	24. VALUE DECLARED (A + B — C)			

Reference	Amount	Rate of exchange

* Where amounts are payable in FOREIGN CURRENCY, indicate in this section the amount in foreign currency and the rate of exchange by reference to each relevant element and item.

† Price actually paid or price payable for settlement at the material time for valuation for customs purposes.

A

Figure 6.7 *Form C105A (reverse)*

EUROPEAN COMMUNITY

4

2 Consignor/*Exporter*	No

1 DECLARATION **A** OFFICE OF DISPATCH/EXPORT

3 Forms	4 Loading lists
5 Items	6 Total packages

Copy for the office of destination

8 Consignee	No

IMPORTANT NOTE

Where this copy is used exclusively for establishing the COMMUNITY STATUS OF GOODS NOT MOVING UNDER THE COMMUNITY TRANSIT PROCEDURE, only the information in boxes 1, 2, 3, 4, 5, 14, 31, 32, 35, 54 and, where appropriate, 33, 38, 40 and 44 is needed for that purpose.

14 Declarant/Representative	No

15 Country of dispatch/*export*

17 Country of destination

18 Identity and nationality of means of transport at departure	19 Ctr

21 Identity and nationality of active means of transport crossing the border

25 Mode of transport at the border	27 Place of loading

4

31 Packages and description of goods	Marks and numbers — Container No(s) — Number and kind	32 Item No	33 Commodity Code

35 Gross mass (kg)

38 Net mass (kg)

40 Summary declaration/Previous document

44 Additional information/ Documents produced/ Certificates and authorisations

A I Code

55 Tranship-ments

Place and country	Place and country
Ident. and nat. new means transp.:	Ident. and nat. new means transp.:
Ctr (1) Identity of new container	Ctr (1) Identity of new container
(1) Enter 1 if YES or 0 if NO	(1) Enter 1 if YES or 0 if NO

F CERTIFI-CATION BY COMPE-TENT AU-THORITIES

New seals: Number: identity:	New seals: Number: identity:
Signature Stamp	Signature Stamp

50 Principal	No	Signature:	**C** OFFICE OF DEPARTURE

51 Intended offices of transit (and country)

represented by

Place and date

52 Guarantee not valid for	Code	53 Office of destination (and country)

D CONTROL BY OFFICE OF DEPARTURE   Stamp

Result

Seals affixed: Number:

identity:

Time limit (date):

Signature:

54 Place and date

Signature and name of declarant/representative

C88 (1-8) Printed in the UK for HMSO 8055017 8/87 G.B.R. F5877 (SEPT 1987)

Figure 6.8 *SAD — status document: used for goods of Community origin (in free circulation)*

Certificate of insurance. This is essential if any claim is to be made by you for loss of or damage to the goods when they arrive. It should show clearly the value for insurance, the risks against which the goods are insured, and be endorsed to you. You always include it in the documents required under a letter of credit.

These are the main 'shipping documents' but there are others, such as *health certificates* required for importing animals or agricultural products, along with *test and inspection certificates* for certain types of goods. Should your supplier ask you for a *delivery specification* or *verification certificate* to prove that the goods he has exported went to the UK, you can get one from HM Customs, after you have completed Form 598 and submitted it to customs.

The despatch of these documents

If the question of payment does not arise then whoever despatches the goods, and insures them etc, will send you the documents you have specified on your order. But because many suppliers link delivery to payment, how you pay often affects how you receive these documents.

First, if you pay cash in advance because your supplier insists, and you have to agree, all the documents are made out to you and sent direct to you by air. Two sets are usually sent in different aircraft.

Second, if you pay on open account, a similar procedure as above is followed, so that you may obtain the goods and then pay as agreed after you have had the goods.

Third, if you pay by documentary letter of credit you specify, when you open the credit, all the documents you wish to be supplied, along with any other shipping conditions you impose. You instruct your bank to tell the advising bank in your supplier's country to accept the documents only if they are exactly as specified and all the conditions of the letter of credit have been satisfied. The advising bank will examine the documents and, if they are correct, will forward them to your bank who will then send them on to you or your import agent. If the documents are incorrect, the advising bank will reject them unless you and your bank agree to amend the terms. In cases like this, the advising bank often sends the documents 'on a collection basis only' which means you have the opportunity to examine the documents and decide whether you will accept them.

Fourth, if your supplier draws a draft on you, he will send all the shipping documents to his bank, who in turn will send them to a bank in the UK. This bank will present you with the draft. If it is payable at sight, as you pay it the bank hands you the documents. If it is payable at a later date, the bank hands you the documents when you accept the draft. Note this applies to shipments by sea, because if the goods are sent by air, road or rail, then delivery is automatic although you still need the other documents to clear the goods at this end.

You should aim to be completely knowledgeable about the documents you need, how many copies you want, how they are to be made out etc, then you will have no problems when the goods arrive in this country. But to ensure all this happens make sure you issue the necessary instructions when you issue the order.

You still, however, have to prepare the customs entries, but we shall deal with this in Chapter 8. Our next task is to look at what duties you can expect to pay, and what reliefs you may be able to claim.

Chapter 7

Duties and Reliefs

When you import goods from overseas you have to clear your goods through customs when they arrive in the UK and to do this you must first know how customs expect you to deal with them.

Dealing with customs

If duties are payable on your imported goods because they are not in free circulation within the EC, or are not entitled to any preferential treatment, or are outside the quota limits, it is your responsibility — or that of your import agent — to present the correct information to HM Customs. You then have four options:

1. You intend to pay the duty and you take away the goods at once.
2. You claim relief from duty, and there are two ways by which relief can be given:
   (a) *Duty suspension*, under which customs duties are not paid when the goods are imported, but security for the duty is given by bond.
   (b) *Reimbursement*, under which the duty is paid at importation, but is paid back when the goods are re-exported following a successful claim for relief. (*Note:* Not for CAP goods — see Notice 221.)
3. You store the goods in what are known as *bonded ware-houses*. These are secure places, privately owned, or belonging to the port authorities. They have two sets of locks on the doors, trader's locks which can only be opened by the trader, and Crown locks which can only be opened by HM Customs staff who are regularly there. Imported goods may be stored under customs control in the ware-house, without payment of duty, and remain there until they are either re-exported, or entered for home use on

payment of the duty. Generally, no manufacturing process is allowed until the goods are released from bond under the supervision of a customs officer, but certain operations are carried out, such as the blending and bottling of whisky. The importance of this warehousing facility to you is that, apart from rent, you can store your goods without tying up your capital in customs duties.

4. You store the goods you have imported in one of the new *freeports* which have the same advantages as bonded warehouses. A freeport is one where no duties are payable when goods enter, and they can leave as they wish. Normally, manufacturing may be carried on there, and customs duties are only payable when goods enter the country, or when they enter another country after being shipped out of the freeport.

The correct procedure with customs is to complete an *entry*, and the type of entry will depend on the end use of the goods. But in normal use there are only about half a dozen forms for entries, which we shall explain in Chapter 8.

You must always advise customs of the nature, quantity, value, origin, internal destination and end use of the goods, to enable them to calculate the duty payable (if any) as well as to decide whether or not to inspect the goods and/or documents. You will now appreciate the importance of your having the correct documents from your suppliers, as we explained in the previous chapter.

In practice, customs select consignments for examination either at random, or for a particular reason, so if they feel that revenue is being prejudiced in any way, they may:

1. Insist on customs duty being paid at once.
2. Hold the goods.
3. Ask for the duty to be covered by a bond or cash deposit, sufficient to pay the maximum duty, which may be refunded or adjusted when the final entry details are accepted and adjusted.

You must remember that, not only have all goods entering the country to be declared to customs, but that they are also liable to physical inspection. If this is required it will be your duty to locate, open and unpack the goods because customs officers will not do this, nor will they accept responsibility for any damage that may occur to the goods during this inspection. You will also have to repack the goods. But in some ports the port authority regulations require all this work to be done by their own employees, who act as your agents for this purpose, and whom you pay for the work.

Your customs entries may be lodged at the appropriate customs office, up to four days before the arrival of the carrying ship or aircraft, and up to seven days after by air and 14 days after by sea. Therefore, you should ask your suppliers to cable or telex the details of the information you will need, in advance of the actual documents. Such information should include the estimated date of arrival of the goods; the name of the ship or flight number of the aircraft; the port of entry; details of the goods, including value and quantity; and if any part shipments have been made. Normally an exporter should do this as part of his duties, but you should specify it on the order.

Customs offices are open during stated hours, but not on Sundays or public holidays. Should you need customs attendance outside these office hours, or at your own premises, a fee is payable. If by any chance goods have not been entered, or have not been cleared, the goods will be sent to a Queen's warehouse at the port. So it is better to make sure that customs formalities are completed as required, and this means using an efficient import agent, as well as making sure your suppliers overseas send you all the information you need, as and when you need it.

Duty

To find out what rates of duty will be charged on your imported goods, you should consult the *Customs Tariff and Overseas Trade Classification*, published by HM Stationery Office. Duties fall into two categories:

1. Fiscal charges, which are excise duties, and these are charged on imported goods at the same rates as for home-produced goods.
2. Customs duties, and agricultural levies arising from the Common Agricultural Policy (CAP) of the European Community.

These customs duties are of various kinds:

(a) Specific, that is a charge of a certain amount per unit of net weight or other measurement of quantity in the tariff.

(b) Ad valorem, that is according to value at the 'quay side', which will be explained below.

(c) Alternative, that is on either (a) or (b) above, whichever is the greater; eg a sewing machine may be charged duty per machine, or on the value of the machine.

(d) Combined, that is containing elements of (a) and (b); eg textiles may be charged duty as a percentage of value, plus the square metre, plus the element of man-made fibre.

(e) There are then anti-dumping and countervailing duties, which are imposed to prevent dumping of cheap goods by foreign countries.

(f) Preferential rates of duty are imposed, as we have seen, for goods which originate in countries with whom the European Community has special arrangements.

(g) Details of the agricultural levies and other CAP charges can be obtained from the Intervention Board for Agricultural Produce (IBAP) at Reading, as set out in Notice 780, 'Import of Goods Subject to the Common Agricultural Policy'.

(h) There are a number of special charges or rebates for certain types of goods such as tobacco, beer, matches, hydrocarbon oil etc, set out in Notice 320.

Customs valuation

Since most goods which are imported pay duty on some form of valuation, it is helpful if you understand what the customs mean by value. This is set out in Section 258 of the Customs and Excise Act of 1952, and is based on what is commonly known as the 'open market' concept. Broadly, it is the price the goods would fetch at the time customs accept the entry, for home use on a sale between buyer and seller, the seller bearing all the costs of freight, insurance, commission and other charges incidental to the sale, and delivery to the buyer.

This customs valuation is explained in *Croner's Reference Book for Importers*, and while it is fairly clear on the question of imports from countries outside the Community, it becomes more complicated when imports are made from other Community countries and countries associated with the Community, because of the series of reliefs which are granted.

The first thing you should note is that imported goods are

valued by customs at the port of entry to the Community, and not their final destination port; eg goods imported into Britain via Le Havre and Southampton can be valued at Le Havre, even though the duty is paid in Southampton. If they came direct to Liverpool they would be valued there. You can see that all expenses and freight of goods after they have first crossed the Community borders are not part of their value for duty, so you need to be able to apportion the amount of EC and non-EC freight costs, especially important when goods come by road. If they come by air, the place for duty valuation is where the common frontier is crossed.

Second, you can of course claim relief from duty for goods which have been imported if they are intended for subsequent re-exportation, but you will need to make a special study of Notices 221, 235, 236 and 770 which deal with these reliefs under EC regulations. The Notices cover goods which are imported for processing; or are exported, then processed and subsequently imported; or are exported and then re-imported as being in 'free circulation'.

While these regulations and the rates of duty payable may seem very complicated, remember you only need to learn them for your own imported goods, and once you have grasped them you need not worry about all the regulations affecting other kinds of imports.

Value added tax

VAT is chargeable on all imported goods whether you are a registered taxable person or not. VAT is not, however, chargeable on imported services. All registered businesses pay VAT on imported goods at the time and place of entry, and the deferment of payment has now been stopped. It can of course be reclaimed in due course.

In some cases VAT may be claimed back, eg on goods which have been re-imported without having undergone any change, or because they are being temporarily imported. Notices 700 and 702 give full particulars. VAT details must be added to customs entry forms.

Duty deferment

If you are an importer or an importer's agent you may defer payment of duty for up to a month on the following:

1. Import duties imposed by or under the Import Duties Act 1958.
2. Anti-dumping and countervailing duties.
3. Levies imposed by or under the Agriculture and Horticulture Act 1964 and the European Economic Communities Act 1972.
4. Sugar surcharge.

You may not claim deferment on the following:

(a) Revenue duties, ie duties on tobacco, beer etc.
(b) Customs charges collected by the postal authorities on delivery of imported postal packages.
(c) Duty and other charges due on importations for which entry is not required, eg baggage.
(d) Duty and other charges subsequently found to be due on goods which were relieved from duty at the time of importation.
(e) Value added tax.

If you wish to claim duty deferment facilities you have to apply to the Collector of Customs and Excise on form C1200, accompanied by a bank guarantee on form C1201, full details being found in Notice 101.

Tariff preference quotas

Nearly all developing countries can, as we have seen, export goods to the UK on a preferential duty basis under the General System of Preference (GSP) system, which means the goods pay less than the normal rate of duty when entering Britain. For most goods originating from the ACP and least developed countries no duty will be payable at all. But for trade 'sensitive' items this preferential duty treatment is limited by quota. This means that when the UK preferential import duty quota for the goods concerned is exhausted, then the full rate of duty is payable. The quota limits for each country are administered separately, except for certain handmade products from 21 specified countries when the quota is treated globally. Full details of the tariff quota system are given in Part II of HM Customs and Excise tariff, and you may also obtain information from the Central Tariff Quota Unit, International Customs Division D, Branch 6, at King's Beam House, Mark Lane, London EC3R 7HE.

To benefit from the preferential rate of duty, whether the goods are subject to quota or not, you must have your supplier send you the appropriate certificate of origin (usually, as you have seen, on GSP Form A or EUR 1). To be eligible for preferential duty the quota works on a first come first served basis until the quota is exhausted. Try to import when the quota is begun, as, for some goods, the quota goes in a matter of days although for others it is never exhausted.

If your imported goods arrive in Britain after the tariff preference quota is exhausted you may store the goods in a customs warehouse, and avoid paying the full duty. You will, however, have to pay storage charges, so you have to work out their cost, and add them to the cost to you of not having the goods, before deciding if it is worth waiting until the new quota comes into force, or if it is better to pay the extra duty involved and import the goods at the non-quota rate.

Where handloom fabrics are concerned eligible goods must have a prescribed certificate of manufacture from a recognised authority in the country of origin. Moreover, each piece of fabric must carry an approved seal at each end, or a single approved lead seal, and the goods must be transported directly from the country of manufacture to Britain.

Least developed countries are given exceptionally favoured import tariff treatment, and are unlikely to be subject to tariff or licensing quotas. You may well feel that importing from these countries would be to your advantage, and they are: Afghanistan, Bangladesh, Botswana, Cape Verde, Ethiopia, Guinea, Guinea Bissau, Haiti, Lesotho, Malawi, Maldives, Nepal, São Tomé and Principe, Sudan, Tanzania, Tonga, Western Samoa, Yemen North and Yemen South, and Burkina Faso.

Once you have established with customs what duties will be payable on the goods you import these will not change appreciably, so you will be able to add duty to your other costs, even though the original calculations may cause you some problems. Your local Customs and Excise Office will always be extremely helpful, and you should not hesitate to consult them if you do not understand the Notices. From practical experience we have found that once customs have decided what has to be paid in the matter of import duty you will experience little difficulty. But to the actual cost of the duty you have still to add the cost of clearing through customs, the subject of the next chapter.

Chapter 8
Clearing Goods Through Customs

In previous chapters we have suggested that you should use the services of an agent to clear your imported goods through customs, as well as arrange for their unloading, and subsequent delivery to you. It is, as we have said, possible for you to do it yourself, but as a small business you will probably be better off using someone else to do the work, especially as you may also need help in having the goods transported to you from overseas. Most freight forwarders combine with their work of shipping goods overseas the inward clearance of goods in Britain. We would emphasise that unless you know a good deal about the procedures for importing you will not be able to brief your agent, and hence you will not necessarily get the best service from him. If that service is poor, your goods will be delayed in arriving and may also be held up by customs.

There are several ways you can find a good import agent. One is to look in *Yellow Pages*. Another is to consult the Institute of Freight Forwarders. You must then detail carefully the services you require: you will probably want the agent to arrange to collect the goods when they arrive in the UK, clear them through customs and deliver them to your premises. You may also want him to collect the goods from your suppliers overseas, and arrange both their transportation and documentation, perhaps insuring them as well. For these services the agent will make a charge, so you must get him to quote in detail the cost of his services. Make sure you have a contract with him, and check up on what he is doing to ensure that you are getting a worthwhile service.

We have so far shown the various import regulations at present in force in some detail; we have covered the shipping documents you are likely to need; we have looked at duties and reliefs you may get from duties; it only remains now to explain how goods are cleared through customs.

Customs entry

The most common form which is used to make customs entries is:

The SAD (Copy 6) which covers all goods imported into the UK.

The Customs Procedure Code (CPC), a 6-digit number, will identify whether the goods are for home use, processing and future re-export etc.

The completion of these entries is explained in Public Notice 465, covering goods imported for home use. The following information is required:

- ☐ Details of any import licence or certificate.
- ☐ The importer's name and address.
- ☐ The consignor's name and address (that is, whoever is sending you the goods).
- ☐ The port or place of importation; the place of discharge and, if necessary, where the goods will be examined.
- ☐ The name and nationality of the carrying ship or airline.
- ☐ Where the goods were loaded overseas.
- ☐ An exact description of the goods, as on your order and as on the invoices etc.
- ☐ The customs tariff item number, ie the HS, Harmonised System of classification, which is the standard classification of goods for customs tariff purposes, now used by most countries and explained on pages 102-3.
- ☐ The quantities of the goods, as required by the tariff.
- ☐ The country of origin and the appropriate code (there is a code for each country that you must use).
- ☐ The country whence the goods were consigned to you and its code (which may be different from the country of origin).
- ☐ The value of the goods for customs purposes, each kind of goods requiring to have a separate value.
- ☐ The duty payable as shown in the schedule. If you claim preferential rates of duty, eg for ACP countries, you must endorse your entry accordingly.
- ☐ Any special surcharges or rebates.
- ☐ The name of the person or company paying the customs duty.
- ☐ The marks and numbers on the consignment.
- ☐ The number and description of packages, the number in words.

EUROPEAN COMMUNITY

6

1 DECLARATION A OFFICE OF DESTINATION

2 Consignor/Exporter   No

3 Forms   4 Loading lists

5 Items   6 Total packages   7 Reference number

Copy for the country of destination

8 Consignee   No

9 Person responsible for financial settlement   No

10 Country last consigned   11 Trad/Prod country   12 Value details   13 CAP

14 Declarant/Representative   No

15 Country of dispatch/export   15 C disp/exp Code a] b]   17 Country destin Code a] b]

16 Country of origin   17 Country of destination

18 Identity and nationality of means of transport on arrival   19 Ctr   20 Delivery terms

21 Identity and nationality of active means of transport crossing the border   22 Currency and total amount invoiced   23 Exchange rate   24 Nature of transaction

25 Mode of transport at the border   26 Inland mode of transport   27 Place of unloading   28 Financial and banking data

6   29 Office of entry   30 Location of goods

31 Packages and description of goods   Marks and numbers — Container No(s) — Number and kind   32 Item No   33 Commodity Code

34 Country origin Code a] b]   35 Gross mass (kg)   36 Preference

37 PROCEDURE   38 Net mass (kg)   39 Quota

40 Summary declaration/Previous document

41 Supplementary units   42 Item price   43 VM Code

44 Additional information/Documents produced/Certificates and authorisations   A1 Code   45 Adjustment

46 Statistical value

47 Calculation of taxes | Type | Tax base | Rate | Amount | MP

48 Deferred payment   49 Identification of warehouse

B ACCOUNTING DETAILS

Total:

50 Principal   No   Signature   C OFFICE OF DEPARTURE

51 Intended offices of transit (and country)   represented by   Place and date:

52 Guarantee not valid for   Code   53 Office of destination (and country)

J CONTROL BY OFFICE OF DESTINATION   54 Place and date

Signature and name of declarant/representative

C88 (1-8)   Printed in the UK for HMSO 8055017 8/87 G.B.R. F5877 (SEPT. 1987)

Figure 8.1 *SAD — import entry*

☐ The bill of lading or air waybill number.
☐ The number of any duty deferment approval.
☐ The liability for VAT and the VAT registration number.

All entries must be made legibly, either typed or written in ballpoint pen. You may take carbon copies (which you always should) and the form must then be signed by you or your import agent. Do not leave any blank spaces, and remember to date the entry. Any corrections must be clearly initialled both on the original and the copies.

Attached to the entry will be a number of supporting documents, of which the chief one will be form C105A or 105B. These forms are used for goods liable for ad valorem duty and valued at over £1300. Remember you have to complete and sign this form, whether you have an import agent or not. If you have bought the goods outright you complete Certificate A, but where the transaction is subject to certain commissions, or similar rights between seller and buyer, then Certificate B is used. So long as the goods are entered within a reasonable time in this latter case, then the value for import duty will be adjusted accordingly.

If you are a regular importer, and this will not apply to most small businesses at first, you should know that instead of completing a number of C105s, you can make a general valuation statement on form C109, in the same way that a large exporter does not have to make individual declarations of exports but can do them together. Should you become large enough to import through the Departmental Entry Processing System (DEPS), you can use form C106 (see below).

In addition you will also need to attach:

1. Some evidence of carriage, eg the appropriate transport document, as we discussed in Chapter 3.
2. Evidence of the freight charges for goods bought on FOB terms, normally shown on the invoices.
3. Extra copies of the invoices if part of a consignment is entered on a different entry.
4. Your authority as the importer to your agent to make any special declarations on your behalf.
5. A work sheet, covering several invoices or tariff item entries.
6. A delivery verification certificate which may be required by your supplier for proving to his government that he has sold the goods to you in the UK.

Then to complete the set of entry documents you will also present the following which will be, or should have been, provided by your supplier:

1. Original invoice, plus at least three copies for customs and VAT.
2. Packing list.
3. Specifications (if necessary).
4. Certificate of origin or form A for GSP treatment.
5. A movement certificate for goods entitled to enter the UK under preferential rates of duty.

If any of these documents are missing then you will have to pay full duties, so you must spend time checking that all documents are ready. We have explained all these documents in previous chapters, and we have also stressed the importance of having your suppliers send you the right documents, with the correct number of copies, as well as the necessity of instructing your suppliers accordingly when you place the order, because exporters are often inaccurate and careless when presenting documents.

Procedures

You take the customs entry and all supporting documents to the Long Room of the Customs House at the port of discharge within the specified period. You normally wait 24 hours before the entry can be collected. You must also pay the correct amount of duty chargeable on imported goods for immediate use, along with the VAT charges.

After this your original entry is sent to the Customs Officer at the docks for comparison with the particulars shown in the Master's report, and for any necessary examination of the goods. Then, if the entry is found correct an 'out of charge' note is issued, and the goods are released. At the same time one copy of the entry will be kept for statistical purposes.

As we have said, examination of goods by customs is random, but you will be told if customs wish to examine your goods, when the procedure will be as shown on page 90.

If an entry is found to be incorrect, the goods are detained by customs until the entry has been rectified and any additional duty paid.

Where goods are to be warehoused, they will be removed from the docks, airport or inland clearance depot (for container shipments) but the revenue will be secured by a bond. This means that some independent company, usually an insurance company, guarantees payment to the customs should the conditions of the bond not be met. If only part of a consignment is withdrawn, the duty is paid as and when the goods are taken.

There are four special procedures of some importance to regular importers:

1. There is a *Triplicate Entry* procedure, which is explained in Notice 461, commonly used for perishable goods at airports which have no customs Long Room facilities (ie facilities for handling entries and duty).
2. At most airports, except London Heathrow and Gatwick, there is a *Transit Shed Register*, used for clearance of consignments up to £600 in value. This means you do not need to complete the usual entry forms, the goods are cleared against a standing deposit, and a register entry used to release the goods. Notice 461 gives the details. There is also the *Simplified Procedure for Import Clearance* for low value goods.
3. There is a *Fast Line* procedure, as set out in Notice 461, designed for goods imported via the short sea routes, where entries cannot be processed before the arrival of the goods, because of the speed at which they reach this country.
4. At major ports and airports customs entries are computer processed. The system is known as DEPS (Departmental Entry Processing System).

Should you begin to import on a regular basis you should always be prepared to discuss with customs how your entry procedures may be improved, because they will consider any reasonable ways of helping you, especially if you have particular problems, eg with perishable goods etc.

Amending entries

You may well have wondered what happens if you make a wrong entry, but discover your mistake only after your original entry has been lodged with customs. You may amend such an entry provided that:

1. The goods have not been cleared.
2. You have not been told the goods are to be examined.
3. Customs have not already discovered the mistake.

If customs discover a mistake involving the underpayment of duty, you will have to complete a supplementary entry known as a 'post' entry, and you will have to pay any additional duty *and* any penalty imposed. If you have overpaid duty, customs will refund this by means of an *over entry certificate.*

The Harmonised Commodity Description and Coding System (HS)

This used to be called the Brussels Tariff or BTN. It was changed to the Customs Co-operation Council Nomenclature (CCCN), and on 1 January 1988 it was enlarged and updated to form the Harmonised System. It is basically a catalogue of all goods traded internationally and will, by 1992, be used by approximately 90 per cent of the world's trading nations.

All products and goods are defined by a numbering system, so that internationally your goods can be identified for customs purposes not by a trade name but by a number.

The Tariff is divided into 21 sections with 97 chapters; for example, Chapter 69 refers to ceramic products which have been fired after shaping. There is a two-tier system of numbering whereby goods coming from the Community will be entered using a nine-digit number, but if they come from outside the Community they will carry an 11-digit number. (There are exceptions to this for goods subject to anti-dumping duty or Common Agricultural Policy products which will have extra digits.)

For example, if you were importing statuettes or other ornamental ceramic articles of porcelain or china, they would be entered as 691310 00 0 if they came from a Community country, but another two digits would have to be added if you were importing from a non-Community country. These extra two digits (The Community Integrated Tariff – TARIC) determine what, if any, duty must be paid. This number should be quoted by you and your suppliers on all documents, so that customs can identify the goods and see exactly what rate of duty is chargeable. You will appreciate that it makes the work of customs all over the world so much easier, while it also prevents arguments as to exactly what rates of duty should apply. From practical experience we suggest you consult customs and get them to agree the exact number under which your imported goods fall, and then quote that number whenever you order. Practically all countries in the world, outside the Communist bloc, use this classification, and while your supplier should be able to pick out the appropriate number this is often not as easy as it sounds. By far the better way, if in any doubt, is for you to get customs to tell you in writing under which heading they consider the products you are importing fall, and then advise everyone concerned of that number.

You will appreciate that there is quite a lot of work required to clear goods through customs and pay the correct duty, as well as benefit from any reliefs to which your goods may be entitled, so you need some help with the customs procedures, as well as having the goods safely delivered to you as quickly as possible with all formalities completed. If you use a good import agent, pay him well, know exactly what you wish him to do, checking to see that he does it accurately and efficiently, then you should experience little difficulty. The cost of using an agent will of course need to be added to all your other expenses, and it is this final landed cost which you will need to know, in order to be able to decide the maximum price you are prepared to pay for the goods.

Chapter 9
How to Be a Professional Importer

By now you will understand that your decision whether to import directly from overseas suppliers, or whether to buy imported goods from agents or companies established in Britain is a most crucial one. If you have decided to buy only from companies which have already imported the goods, then this involves you in no more work than dealing with any domestic supplier. If, however, you decide to buy some or all of your imported goods directly from suppliers overseas, in order to obtain the full advantage such importing brings in the form of lower prices, higher profits, and generally better treatment from the overseas suppliers (as we suggested in Chapter 1), you will need to become a highly professional importer. This is because you will be dealing with highly professional exporters, who will be out to sell to you at their highest prices, on their best terms of payment, aiming to make the very most of their sales to you. Your task is to buy at the lowest possible prices, on the best payment terms for yourself, and thus make the highest profits you can, when the goods arrive in the UK.

Exporting is taught to people all over the world because it is considered to be in the interests of a nation. It is explained simply in *Export for the Small Business* by Henry Deschampsneufs, also published by Kogan Page. Importing, however, is not so well taught because it is not often considered to be in a nation's interest, so exporters tend to think they can get the better of importers. If you, as an importer, allow this to happen you will lose many or all of the advantages of being a direct importer. To prevent this happening, you should:

1. Be quite clear what you wish to buy, because you already know exactly what you can do with the goods when you get them.
2. Identify the best sources of supply wherever they happen to be in the world.
3. Figure out all your costs and then arrive at a price and

    terms which will give you the best margin of profit when you resell or use the imported goods.

4. Handle the transport, insurance and documentation of the goods or have it efficiently handled for you.
5. Cope with payment problems in such a way that you, as the customer, benefit most.
6. Handle, or have handled for you, all the entry procedures including customs clearance when the goods arrive in the UK.
7. Obtain quotations which overseas suppliers are eager to fulfil, because they reckon you to be an importer of some standing.
8. Issue orders which are explicit, so there is no possibility of any breach of contract, and your suppliers know exactly what you wish them to do.
9. Negotiate the best possible terms for yourself from your suppliers.

It is our hope that what you have read in this book will enable you to develop a highly professional attitude to importing, and that you will do it as efficiently as you do any other part of your business.

If you buy from overseas you can either use what you buy or resell it for someone else to use. If you buy to resell you can, of course, also act as an agent or distributor of the supplier in the UK, but you must be clear what you will do with the goods before you import them. It is not always easy to be a good buyer, but you will have learned the pitfalls in your domestic business.

Identifying sources of supply will be your next major problem and we have already suggested some ways in which you can do this. Ultimately, of course, you will need to travel overseas, partly to find the most suitable sources of supply and partly to obtain the best terms. While travelling around the world is not difficult these days, there is a great deal of difference between doing it well and doing it badly. For example, you should use a good travel agent to get the cheapest fares. Having hotel accommodation booked and available is as necessary as having flights booked in advance. You will need advice on when to visit countries, where to stay, what clothing to take, how long to be there, what currency you need, and how to get around the city or country you are in. A good agent should be able to help, but also consult the 'Hints to Exporters' booklets published by the British Overseas Trade Board.

From much practical experience we suggest you plan your visits overseas with great care. You should make appointments with key people in advance to ensure they will be able to see you. You should leave time for unexpected contacts. You should take with you all estimates of costs and therefore of the prices you are prepared to pay. You should know what quantities would be suitable, and when you would place the orders, along with the terms and methods of payment to which you would agree, since all these, as we have shown, affect the price you can afford to pay. The more homework you do the better, so you are not mesmerised by some smart, slick export salesman overseas.

Throughout this book we have continually emphasised the importance of knowing the total cost of the goods you import. This cost is often referred to as your *landed cost* and consists of:

The price paid to the exporter or supplier.
Transportation (if not included in the price).
Insurance (if not included in the price).
Documentation (if you have incurred any costs yourself).
Landing charges.
VAT.
Customs duties.
Inland transport.
Clearing and handling charges.

To the above you must then add, first, any costs involved in paying for the goods, such as the costs of opening a letter of credit etc, as set out in Chapter 4. Second, you must include a proportion of your fixed overhead costs. Third, you must allow for the use of the money. Fourth, you must include any specific expenditure incurred in importing, such as a visit to the country concerned. There will be a great deal of figure work connected with importing, and in our experience most importers spend half their time on finances, a quarter on staff, and the remaining quarter on buying and selling.

For most small businesses the secret of efficient transport, insurance, documentation and clearance of goods through customs etc rests with a good import agent. But this in turn depends on your efficiency and knowledge as to what has to be done, while the secret of good buying will be linked to the way you request quotations and hand out orders.

Negotiating depends on being able to deal with the seller so that you get your fair share of the bargain. You must give a little but you must see that your seller also gives. Remember that you cannot decide a price until you can say when you will buy, in what quantities and how and when you will pay. You should always have a maximum price beyond which you will not deal, and hope to be able to buy at less than this price. You must learn to bargain both by correspondence and in person. You must learn the idiosyncrasies of your buyers, and the different habits, customs and ways of doing business in various countries. So study your suppliers, and trade or bargain with them as they would wish — that is the way to get the best deals out of them.

Remember that, as a buyer, the initiative is with you. You decide whether to buy or not. You must always retain that initiative, being clear and decisive as to what you buy, when you buy, how much you buy and how you will pay.

Above all, enjoy importing. The way to enjoy it is to do it efficiently and, therefore, profitably; and you may then truly call yourself a professional importer.

Appendix 1
Useful Addresses

UK Chambers of Commerce

Aberdeen
Aberdeen Chamber of Commerce
15 Union Terrace
Aberdeen AB9 1HF
0224 29222

Ashford, Kent
London Chamber Ashford Office
Ashford House
Tufton Centre
Ashford TN23 1YB
0233 39562

Ayr
Ayr Chamber of Commerce
Royal Bank Buildings
28 Sandgate
Ayr KA7 1BS
0292 65004

Barking
London Chamber Barking and Dagenham Office
(Documentation only)
20 Cambridge Road
Barking IG11 8NW
01-594 3195

Barnsley
Barnsley and District Chamber of Commerce
12 Victoria Road
Barnsley S70 2BB
0226 83131

Belfast
Northern Ireland Chamber of Commerce and Industry
22 Great Victoria Street
Belfast BT2 7BJ
0232 244113

Birkenhead
Wirrall Chamber of Commerce
26 Hamilton Square
Birkenhead L41 6DF
051-647 8085

Birmingham
Birmingham Chamber of Industry and Commerce
PO Box 360
75 Harborne Road
Birmingham B15 3DH
021-454 6171

Blackburn
Blackburn and District Incorporated Chamber of Industry and Commerce
14 Richmond Terrace
Blackburn BB1 7BH
0254 664747

Bolton
Bolton Chamber of Commerce and Industry
Silverwell House
Silverwell Street
Bolton BL1 1PX
0204 33896

Boston
Boston and District Chamber of Commerce
5 South Square
Boston PE21 6JA
0205 62267

Bradford
Bradford Chamber of Commerce
Commerce House
Cheapside
Bradford BD1 4JZ
0274 728166

Brighton
**Federation of Sussex Industries
and Chamber of Commerce**
Seven Dials Corner
Brighton BN1 3JS
0273 26282

Bristol
**Bristol Chamber of Commerce
and Industry**
16 Clifton Park
Bristol BS8 3BY
0272 737373

Burnley
**Burnley and District Incorporated
Chamber of Commerce and Industry**
16 Keirby Walk
Burnley BB11 2DE
0282 36555

Burton upon Trent
**Burton upon Trent and District
Chamber of Commerce and Industry**
158 Derby Street
Burton upon Trent DE14 2NZ
0283 63761

Bury
**Bury and District Chamber
of Commerce**
Castle Chambers
Market Place
Bury BL9 0LD
061-764 8640

Cambridge
**Cambridge and District Chamber
of Commerce and Industry**
Owen Webb House
1 Gresham Road
Cambridge CB1 2EP
0223 355713

Cardiff
**Cardiff Chamber of Commerce
and Industry**
101-8 The Exchange
Mount Stuart Square
Cardiff CF1 6RD
0222 481648

Carlisle
Carlisle Chamber of Commerce
20 Spencer Street
Carlisle CA1 1BG
0228 26288

Chatham
**Medway and Gillingham
Chamber of Commerce**
149 New Road
Chatham ME4 4PT
0634 408344

Chester
**Chester and North Wales
Chamber of Commerce**
6 Hunter Street
Chester CH1 2AU
0244 23051

Chesterfield
**Chesterfield and District
Chamber of Commerce**
57-9 Saltergate
Chesterfield S40 1UL
0246 203456

Colchester
**Colchester and District
Chamber of Trade and Commerce**
5 High Street
Colchester CO1 1DA
0206 65277

Coventry
**Coventry Chamber of
Commerce and Industry**
123 St Nicholas Street
Coventry CV1 4FD
0203 51777

Crawley
**London Chamber of
Commerce and Industry**
22 The Boulevard
Crawley RH10 1WP
0293 30017

Croydon
Croydon Chamber of Commerce
Commerce House
21 Scarbrook Road
Croydon CR9 6HY
01-681 7770/2165

Derby
**Derby and Derbyshire Chamber
of Commerce and Industry**
4 Vernon Street
Derby DE1 1FR
0332 47031

Doncaster
Doncaster Chamber of Commerce
7-8 Winchester House
Scot Lane
Doncaster DN1 1EX
0302 61947

Douglas, Isle of Man
**Isle of Man Chamber of Trade,
Commerce and Industry**
6 St George's Street
Douglas
0624 4941

Dudley
**Dudley Chamber of Industry
and Commerce**
Falcon House
The Minories
Dudley DY2 8P8
0384 237653

Dundee
**Dundee and Tayside Chamber
of Commerce and Industry**
Chamber of Commerce Buildings
Panmure Street
Dundee DD1 1ED
0382 22122

Edinburgh
**Edinburgh Chamber of Commerce
and Manufacturers**
Leith Chamber of Commerce
3 Randolph Crescent
Edinburgh EH3 7UD
031-225 5851

Exeter
**Exeter and District Chamber
of Commerce and Trade**
Equitable Life House
31 Southernhay East
Exeter EX1 1NS
0392 36641

Falkirk
**Central Scotland Chamber
of Commerce**
11 Orchard Street
Falkirk FK1 1RF
0324 22280

Glasgow
Glasgow Chamber of Commerce
30 George Square
Glasgow G2 1EQ
041-204 2121

Gloucester
**Gloucester and County
Chamber of Commerce**
20 Cheltenham Road
Gloucester GL2 0LS
0452 23383

Goole
**Goole and District Chamber
of Commerce and Shipping**
13 Dunhill Road
Goole DN14 6SS
0405 69164

Grantham
Grantham Chamber of Commerce
Harlaxton Road
Grantham NG31 7SF
0476 66301

Great Yarmouth
**Great Yarmouth Chamber
of Commerce**
2 South Quay
Great Yarmouth NR30 2QH
0493 2184

Greenford
London Chamber Ealing Office
6 Ruislip Road
Greenford, Middlesex
01-575 3542

Greenock
Greenock Chamber of Commerce
73 Union Street
Greenock PA16 8BG
0475 20175, 25105

Grimsby
**Grimsby and Immingham Chamber
of Commerce and Shipping**
Yorkshire Bank Chambers
West St Mary's Gate
Grimsby DN31 1LA
0472 42981

Guernsey, CI
Guernsey Chamber of Commerce
10 Grange
St Peter Port
Guernsey, CI
0481 27483

Halifax
**Calderdale Chamber of Commerce
and Industry**
36 Clare Road
Halifax HX1 2HX
0422 52517

Hatfield
**Hertfordshire Chamber
of Commerce**
Andre House
Salisbury Square
Hatfield AL9 5BH
07072 72771, 72441

Hawick
**South of Scotland
Chamber of Commerce**
19 Buccleuch Street
Hawick TD9 0HL
0450 72267

High Wycombe
**South Bucks and East Berks
Chamber of Commerce and Industry**
Buckingham House
Desborough Road
High Wycombe HP11 2PR
0494 445909

Huddersfield
**Kirklees and Wakefield Chamber
of Commerce and Industry**
Commerce House
New North Road
Huddersfield HD1 5PJ
0484 26591

Hull
**Hull Incorporated Chamber
of Commerce and Shipping**
Samman House
Bowlalley Lane
Hull HU1 1XT
0482 24976

Ipswich
**Ipswich and Suffolk Chamber
of Commerce and Shipping**
21 Museum Street
Ipswich IP1 1HE
0473 210611
Telex 987703

Isle of Wight
**Isle of Wight Chamber of
Commerce**
6-7 Town Lane
Newport PO30 1NR
0983 524390

Jersey, CI
**Jersey Chamber of Commerce
and Industry**
19 Royal Square
St Helier
Jersey, CI
0534 24536, 71031

Kendal
**Kendal and District Incorporated
Chamber of Commerce and
Manufacturers**
Exchange Chambers
10B Highgate
Kendal
0539 20049

Kidderminster
**Kidderminster and District
Chamber of Commerce**
Duke Place
Kidderminster DY10 2JR
0562 515515

Kirkcaldy
**Kirkcaldy and District
Chamber of Commerce**
288 High Street
Kirkcaldy KY1 1LB
0592 201932

Lancaster
**Lancaster District Chamber of
Commerce, Trade and Industry**
St Leonard's House
St Leonardgate
Lancaster LA1 1NN
0524 39467

Leeds
**Leeds Chamber of Commerce
and Industry**
Commerce House
2 St Alban's Place
Leeds LS2 8HZ
0532 430491

Leicester
**Leicester and County Chamber
of Commerce and Industry**
4th Floor, York House
91 Granby Street
Leicester LE1 6EA
0533 551491

Lincoln
Lincoln Chamber of Commerce
15-16 St Mary's Street
Lincoln LN5 7EQ
0522 23713

Liverpool
**Merseyside Chamber of
Commerce and Industry**
1 Old Hall Street
Liverpool L3 9HG
051-227 1234

London postal area
**London Chamber of Commerce
and Industry**
69 Cannon Street
London EC4N 5AB
01-248 4444

**London Chamber Cricklewood
Office**
303-15 Cricklewood Broadway
London NW2 6PQ
01-450 3575

**City of Westminster Chamber
of Commerce**
Mitre House
177 Regent Street
London W1R 8DJ
01-734 2851

**Hammersmith and Fulham
Chamber of Commerce**
4 King Street
London W6 0QA
01-748 1893

Londonderry
**Londonderry Chamber of
Commerce**
1-3 Clarendon Street
Londonderry BT48 7EP
0504 62379

Lowestoft
Lowestoft Chamber of Commerce
36 Loxley Road
Oulton Broad
Lowestoft NR33 9PG
0502 2286

Luton
**Luton, Bedford and District
Chamber of Commerce
and Industry**
Commerce House
Stuart Street
Luton LU1 5AU
0582 23456, 416943

Manchester
**Manchester Chamber of
Commerce and Industry**
56 Oxford Street
Manchester M60 7HJ
061-236 3210

Middlesbrough
**Teesside and District Chamber
of Commerce and Industry**
Commerce House
Marton Road
Middlesbrough TS1 1DW
0642 230023

Milton Keynes
**Milton Keynes and District
Chamber of Commerce
and Industry**
668 North Row
Lloyds Court
Secklow Gate West
Central Milton Keynes MK9 3AP
0908 662123

Neath
**Neath, Briton Ferry and District
Chamber of Commerce**
17 Elm Road
Briton Ferry
Neath SA11 2LY
0639 820269

Newark
Newark and District Chamber
of Commerce and Industry
3 Middle Gate
Newark NG24 1AQ
0636 71881

Newcastle upon Tyne
Tyne and Wear Chamber
of Commerce and Industry
65 Quayside
Newcastle upon Tyne NE1 3DS
0632 611142

Newhaven
Newhaven and District Chamber
of Commerce
51 High Street
Newhaven BN9 9PA
07912 3307

Newport, Gwent
Newport and Gwent Chamber
of Commerce
Carlton Chambers
High Street
Newport NPT 1GE
0633 58509

Newport, Isle of Wight
Isle of Wight Chamber
of Commerce
6-7 Town Lane
Newport PO30 1NR
0983 524390

Northampton
Northamptonshire Chamber
of Commerce and Industry
65 The Avenue
Cliftonville
Northampton NN1 5BG
0604 22422

Norwich
Norwich and Norfolk Chamber
of Commerce and Industry
112 Barrack Street
Norwich NR3 1UB
0603 25977, 25992

Nottingham
Nottingham Chamber of
Commerce and Industry
395 Mansfield Road
Nottingham NG5 2DL
0602 624624

Oldham
Oldham and District
Chamber of Commerce
94 Werneth Hall Road
Oldham OL8 4AX
061-624 2482

Oxford
Oxford and District
Chamber of Commerce
4 Bank Court Chambers
Cowley Centre
Oxford OX4 3YF
0865 772255

Paisley
Paisley Chamber of
Commerce and Industry
51 Moss Street
Paisley PA1 1DS
041-889 6244

Perth
Perthshire Chamber of Commerce
16 Dunkeld Road
Perth PH1 5RW
0738 37626

Plymouth
Plymouth Chamber of Commerce
and Industry
29 Looe Street
Plymouth PL4 0EE
0752 21151

Poole
Dorset Chamber of Commerce
and Industry
Old Victoria Mills
The Quay
Poole BH15 1HY
0202 682000

Portsmouth
South-East Hampshire Chamber
of Commerce and Industry
27 Guildhall Walk
Portsmouth PO1 2RP
0705 825351

Port Talbot
**Port Talbot Chamber of
Commerce and Shipping**
1 Beechwood Road
Port Talbot SA13 2AD
0639 884429

Preston
**Central and West Lancashire
Chamber of Commerce and
Industry**
2 Camden Place
Preston PR1 8BE
0772 555246, 556261

Reading
**Reading Chamber of Commerce
and Trade**
43 West Street
Reading RG1 7AT
0734 595049

Rochdale
**Rochdale and District Chamber
of Commerce**
County Court Building
Town Hall Square
Rochdale OL16 1NF
0706 343810

Rotherham
Rotherham Chamber of Commerce
37 Moorgate Road
Rotherham S60 2AE
0709 2001

Rugby
**Rugby and District Chamber
of Commerce**
9 Railway Terrace
Rugby CV21 3EN
0788 4951

Runcorn
Halton Chamber of Commerce
57-61 Church Street
Runcorn WA7 1LG
09285 60958

Scunthorpe
**Scunthorpe, Glanford and
Gainsborough Chamber
of Commerce**
58 Oswald Road
Scunthorpe DN15 7PQ
0724 842109

Sheffield
Sheffield Chamber of Commerce
Commerce House
33 Earl Street
Sheffield S1 3FX
0742 730114

Shetland
Shetland Chamber of Commerce
122 Commercial Street
Lerwick ZE1 0HX
0595 4739 (telephone between
1.30 and 3.30 pm Monday-Friday)

Slough
**South Bucks and East Berks
Chamber of Commerce and Industry**
2-6 Bath Road
Slough SL1 3SB
0753 77877

Southampton
**Southampton Chamber of
Commerce**
Bugle House
53 Bugle Street
Southampton SO9 4WP
0703 23541

Stockport
**Stockport Chamber of
Commerce and Industry**
Borough Chambers
St Petersgate
Stockport SK1 1EE
061-480 0321

Stoke-on-Trent
**North Staffordshire Chamber
of Commerce and Industry**
Commerce House
Festival Park
Stoke-on-Trent ST1 5BE
0782 202222

Swansea
**Swansea Chamber of Commerce
and Shipping**
Rooms F6/F7
Burrows Chambers
East Burrows Road
Swansea SA1 1RF
0792 53297

Swindon
Swindon Chamber of Commerce
1-2 Commercial Road
Swindon SN1 5NE
0793 616544

Telford
**Telford and Shropshire Chamber
of Industry and Commerce**
Walker House
Telford Centre
Telford TF3 4HA ›
0952 502535, 502560

Tunbridge Wells
**Royal Tunbridge Wells Chamber
of Trade**
56 Mount Ephraim Road
Tunbridge Wells PN1 1EJ
0892 46888

Wakefield
**Kirklees and Wakefield Chamber
of Commerce and Industry**
12 Rishworth Street
Wakefield WF1 3BY
0924 376103

Walsall
**Walsall Chamber of Commerce
and Industry**
Chamber of Commerce House
Ward Street
Walsall WS1 2AG
0922 647209

Warrington
**Warrington Chamber of
Commerce and Industry**
3 Springfield Street
Warrington WA1 1BD
0925 35054

Westcliff-on-Sea
**Southend Chamber of Commerce,
Trade and Industry**
Commerce House
845 London Road
Westcliff-on-Sea SS0 9SZ
0702 77090

Wigan
**Wigan and District Incorporated
Chamber of Commerce**
25 Bridgeman Terrace
Wigan WN1 1TD
0942 496074

Wolverhampton
**Wolverhampton Chamber of
Commerce and Industry**
Berrington Lodge
93 Tettenhall Road
Wolverhampton WV3 9PE
0902 26726

Worcester
**Worcester and Hereford Area
Chamber of Commerce
and Indsutry**
10 The Moors
Worcester WR1 3EE
0905 611611

Foreign trade associates and overseas Chambers of Commerce in London

American Chamber of Commerce
75 Brook Street
London W1Y 2EB
01-493 0381

Arab-British Chamber of Commerce
26A Albemarle Street
London W1A 4BL
01-499 3400

**Australian-British Trade
Association**
6th Floor
Dorland House
18-20 Lower Regent Street
London SW1Y 4PW
01-930 2524

**Belgo-Luxembourg Chamber
of Commerce**
36-7 Piccadilly
London W1V 0PL
01-434 1815

Brazilian Chamber of Commerce
35 Dover Street
London W1X 3RA
01-499 0186

**British Overseas Trade Group for
Israel**
Michael House
Baker Street
London W1A 1DN
01-935 4422

**British-Soviet Chamber of
Commerce**
2 Lowndes Street
London SW1X 9ET
01-235 2423

Canada UK Chamber of Commerce
3 Lower Regent Street
London SW1Y 4NZ
01-930 2794

French Chamber of Commerce
54 Conduit Street
London W1R 9SD
01-439 1735

**German Chamber of Industry
and Commerce**
12-13 Suffolk Street
London SW1Y 4HG
01-930 7251

**Hong Kong Trade Development
Council**
8 St James's Square
London SW1Y 4JZ
01-930 7955

Italian Chamber of Commerce
Walmer House
296 Regent Street
London W1R 6AE
01-637 3153

**Netherlands-British Chamber
of Commerce**
Dutch House
307-8 High Holborn
London WC1V 7LS
01-242 1064

Miscellaneous addresses

British Importers Confederation
69 Cannon Street
London EC4N 5AB
01-248 4444

British Overseas Trade Board
1 Victoria Street
London SW1H 0ET
01-215 7877

British Standards Institution
2 Park Street
London W1A 2BS
01-629 9000

Central Office of Information
Hercules Road
London SE1 7DU
01-928 2345

Croner Publications Ltd
Croner House
173 Kingston Road
New Malden
Surrey KT3 3SS
01-942 8966
For details of *Croner's Reference
Book for Importers*, loose-leaf
binder available on subscription,
with monthly updates.

Customs Statistical Office
HM Customs and Excise
Portcullis House
27 Victoria Avenue
Southend-on-Sea
Essex
0802 49421

Department of Trade and Industry
Duty Remissions Branch
General Division
Kingsgate House
1 Victoria Street
London SW1E 0ET
01-215 7877
Duty remissions.

Department of Trade and Industry
Import Licensing Branch
Charles House,
375 Kensington High Street
London W14 8QH
01-603 4644
Import licences.

Department of Trade and Industry
Consumer Affairs
Fair Trading Division
Millbank Tower
London SW1P 4QU
01-211 3204
Marking of goods.

HM Customs and Excise
Headquarters
King's Beam House
Mark Lane
London EC3R 7HE
01-626 1515

HM Stationery Office
PO Box 276
London SW85 5DT
01-928 6977 ext 345
For details of subscription to
British Business, a weekly magazine
giving import, export and industrial
news from the Department of
Trade and Industry.

Institute of Freight Forwarders
Suffield House
9 Paradise Road
Richmond
Surrey TW9 1SA
01-948 3141

Intervention Board for Agricultural Produce
Fountain House
2 Queens Walk
Reading
Berkshire RG1 7QW
0734 583626

Simplification of International Trade Procedures Board (SITPRO)
Almack House
26-8 King Street
London SW1Y 6QW
01-930 0532
A government department
concerned with making the
paperwork involved in international
trade less complicated.

Statistics and Market Intelligence Library
1 Victoria Street
London SW1H 0ET
01-215 5444

Appendix 2
Public Notices with Useful Information for Importers

All public notices are available free of charge from HM Customs and Excise.

Appendix 3
Commonly Used Abbreviations

A-BCC Arab-British Chamber of Commerce
ACP African, Caribbean and Pacific group of countries
A/D all-risks
ADR European Agreement on the International Carriage of Dangerous Goods by Road
Ad Val ad valorem
ATA Carnet international customs document (covering temporary duty-free and tax-free entry of specified goods)
ATP Agreement on the International Carriage of Perishable Foodstuffs
AWB air waybill
B/Ex bill of exchange
B/L bill of lading
BOTB British Overseas Trade Board
BOTGI British Overseas Trade Group for Israel
BSI British Standards Institution
BTN Brussels Tariff Number (see also CCCN and TTCN); replaced by HS
CAD cash against documents
C & E Customs and Excise
C & F cost and freight
CAP Common Agricultural Policy
CBI Confederation of British Industry
CCCN Customs Co-operation Council Nomenclature (see also BTN and TTCN); replaced by HS
CCT Common Customs Tariff
Cert Ins certificate of insurance
C/I consular invoice
CIF cost, insurance and freight
CIM international convention on the transport of goods by railway
CMR international convention covering transport of goods by road
C/O certificate of origin
COI Central Office of Information
Comecon Council of Mutual Economic Assistance (the state-trading countries)
COMET Committee for Middle East Trade
CPA claims payable abroad
CT Community tariff
CTC customs transaction code — identifies on the customs entry form the end-use of the imported goods
CVO certificate of value and origin
D/A documents against acceptance
DDP delivered duty paid
D/P documents against payment

120

EC European Community

ECU European currency unit (see also UA) — a unit of financial measurement within the EC. The pound sterling will be fixed at so many units on a specific date as will all the other European currencies in the 'currency basket'.

EFTA European Free Trade Association

FAS free alongside ship

FCL full container load

FOB free on board

FOQ free on quay

FOR free on rail

FOT free on truck

FRANCO 'free delivered'

FRC free on carrier

FTA free trade area

G/A general average

GATT General Agreement on Tariffs and Trade

GSP Generalised System of Preferences — whereby goods from developing countries are given preferential tariff treatment

HS Harmonised System of Classification

IATA International Air Transport Association

IBAP Intervention Board for Agricultural Produce

ICAO International Civil Aviation Organisation

ICC International Chamber of Commerce

ICD inland clearance depot

IMF International Monetary Fund

Incoterms International Chamber of Commerce rules for the interpretation of trade terms

IPR inward processing relief

L/C letter of credit

LCL less than a container load

LIC local import control

MCA Monetary Compensatory Amount — refunds under the CAP

MFA Multi-Fibre Arrangement — regulates international trade in textile and clothing; imports will be subject to quota limits

MFN most favoured nation treatment in a commercial treaty between two or more countries guarantees that all parties in the agreement will automatically extend to each other any trade concession they might subsequently give to non-member countries

MT mail transfer

OCT overseas countries and territories

OECD Organisation for Economic Co-operation and Development

OGL open general licence

Ro-Ro roll-on, roll-off

SITPRO Simplification of International Trade Procedures Board

SWIFT Society of Worldwide International Financial Telecommunications

TDC total distribution cost concept

TIR Transport International Routier carnet

TT telegraphic transfer

TTCN Tariff Trade Code Numbers; replaced by HS

UA units of account (see also ECU)

W/M weight/measurement

Appendix 4
Further Reading from Kogan Page

Kogan Page publish an extensive list of books for small and medium-sized businesses; those particularly helpful to the reader of this book are likely to be:

Be Your Own Company Secretary, A J Scrine, 1987
The Business Fact Finder, editor Hano Johannsen, 1987
Buying for Business: How to Get a Good Deal from Your Suppliers, Tony Attwood, 1988
Choosing and Using Professional Advisers, editor Paul Chaplin, 1986
Effective Advertising: The Daily Telegraph Guide for the Small Business, H C Carter, 1986
Export for the Small Business, Henry Deschampsneufs, 1984
Financial Management for the Small Business, 2nd edition, Colin Barrow, 1988
Getting Sales: A Practical Guide to Getting More Sales for Your Business, R D Smith and G M Dick, 1986
How to Buy a Business: The Daily Telegraph Guide, Peter Farrell, 1983
How to Choose Business Premises: A Guide for the Small Firm, Howard Green, Brian Chalkley and Paul Foley, 1986
How to Deal With Your Bank Manager, Geoffrey Sales, 1988
Law for the Small Business: The Daily Telegraph Guide, 5th edition, Patricia Clayton, 1987
A Manager's Guide to Patents, Trade Marks and Copyright, John F Williams, 1986
Raising Finance: The Guardian Guide for the Small Business, 2nd edition, Clive Woodcock, 1985
So You Think Your Business Needs a Computer? Khalid Aziz, 1986
The Stoy Hayward Business Tax Guide, annual
Successful Expansion for the Small Business: The Daily Telegraph Guide, M J Morris, 1985
Successful Marketing for the Small Business: The Daily Telegraph Guide, Dave Patten, 1985
Taking Up a Franchise: The Daily Telegraph Guide, 4th edition, Colin Barrow and Godfrey Golzen, 1987

Index